SHAKEN NOT STIRRED

SHAKEN NOT STIRRED

A CELEBRATION
OF THE MARTINI

ANISTATIA R. MILLER & JARED M. BROWN

WILLIAM MORROW
An Imprint of HarperCollinsPublishers

FIRST EDITION

Designed by Anistatia R. Miller and Jared M. Brown

Library of Congress Cataloging-in-Publication Data has been applied for.

ISBN 978-0-06-213026-6

13 14 15 16 17   DIX/RRD   10 9 8 7 6 5 4 3 2 1

CONTENTS

THE MARTINI MENU

(Note: For a key to the icon used throughout this book, see page 207.)

CLASSIC GIN MARTINIS

3Ds Martini	55
American Martini Cocktail	55
Antlers Dirty Gibson	61
Arnaud Martini	73
Astoria Cocktail, The	77
Beefsteak Martini	92
Berlin Station Chief, The	83
Bijou Cocktail	50
Boomerang Cocktail	80
Boulevard Cocktail	72
Bradford à la Martini	50
Bronx Cocktail	72
Bronx Express	72
Cardinale	87
Chorus Lady	72
Classic Gin Martini	50
Cock-tail (vulgarly called "ginger")	38
Cooperstown	87
Corpse Reviver #2	71
Crist Cocktail, The	50
Dempsey, The	97
Diplomatic Martini	82
Dirty Gibson	64
Dirty Martini	75
Dry Martini Cocktail	54
Dusty Martini	72
Fairbanks Cocktail	70
Fallen Angel	72
Fancy Gin Cocktail	46
Fifty-Fifty	58
Fitty-Fitty	57
Fourth Estate	69
French Reverse Martini	82
Gibson Cocktail	61
Gin Cocktail	46
Gloom Raiser	69
Godfrey's Corpse Reviver	98
Golden Triangle Station Chief	83
Green Park Cocktail	98
H.P.W.	50
Hanky-Panky Cocktail	69
Hawksmoor Martini	56
Hoffman House Cocktail	53
Klondike Cocktail	53
Knickerbocker Cocktail	59
Knickerbocker Dry Oliver Twist	60
Leospo Cocktail	55
Madeira Martinez	46
Marguerite Cocktail (Johnson)	52
Marguerite Cocktail (Muckensturm)	53
Marguerite Cocktail (Stuart)	51
Martinez	45
Martini Cocktail #1	55
Martini Cocktail (Fouquet)	50
Martini Cocktail (Johnson)	47
Martini Cocktail (Kappeler)	58
Martini Cocktail Dry	55
Martini Verboten	44
Martini's Martini	43
Medium Martini	80
Miss Molly	52
Montgomery, The	79
Murphy Cocktail	64
Old Army Cocktail, The	62
Original Martini Cocktail	55
Paisley Cocktail	83
Pall Mall Cocktail	80
Paraguay Station Chief	83
Parisian Martini (aka: Arnaud Martini)	73
Pebble Martini	50
Perfect Cocktail	60
Perfect Martini	80
Pink Gin	41
Plaza Cocktail	78
Princeton Cocktail (post-Prohibition)	68
Princeton Cocktail	68
Racquet Club Cocktail	50
Ransom Martinez	46
Reverse Martini, The (Child)	81
Reverse Martini (Harding)	82
Rolls-Royce Cocktail	70
Royal Wedding	83
Savoy Hotel Special Cocktail (No. 1)	78
Savoy Hotel Special Cocktail (No. 2)	78
Shinkansen Martini	62
Spring Forward	64
Star Cocktail (Nassau Gun Club)	74
Star Cocktail, The	74
Super-Dry Virgin Martini	84
Sweet Martini Cocktail for Ladies	56
Sweet Martini Cocktail	56
Trilby Cocktail	74
Trilby Cocktail (Johnson)	74
Turf Cocktail	53
Twentieth-Century Cocktail	71
Virgin Martini, The	84
Will Rogers Cocktail	72
Yale Cocktail	65
Yellow Rattler	70

CLASSIC VODKA MARTINIS

Argentine-Arctic Kick, The	113
Beso de Cosaco	99

Burns Straight Up	102	Cosmopolitan (Cook)	147
Club Martini	111	Cosmopolitan (DeGroff)	147
Dempsey Cocktail	96	Cosmopolitan (Dunsworth)	147
Devil's Torch	98	Cosmopolitan (Huffman/Cecchini)	147
Direct Martini	109	Cosmopolitan Daisy	148
Dreamy Dorini Smoking Martini	119	Eclipse Martini	148
From Russia with Love	106	Fresh Fruit Martini	144
Hittite Cocktail, The	99	Golden Apple Martini	143
Iron Curtain Cocktail	98	Kamikaze Cocktail	148
Joe Average	108	Lemon Drop	152
Lenna Cocktail	101	Lemon Drop #2	152
Little Tickle Cocktail	101	Lemon Drop #3	152
Lucky Jim	108	Lola	140
Lucky Martini	103	Lola Granitée	141
Mariner's Martini	116	Lychee Martini #2	145
Molotov Cocktail	118	Lychee Martini	145
Nairn Falls	114	Metropolitan	147
Nervo-Knox Cocktail	101	Palace Apple Skyy	143
Octopus Martini	116	Porn Star Martini	153
Octopus's Garden Martini	116	Pumpkin Martini	151
Oliver's Classic Martini	117	Raspberry Martini	145
Red Vesper	106	Red Caramel Apple Martini	143
Royal Toast Cocktail	103	Spider Bite, The	175
S.O.S., The	101	Watermelon Martini	145
Seattle, The	109	William Tell	143
Smoked Martini	119	Woo Woo	148
Tatouni, The	108		
Thunderer, The	105		
Thyme Vesper	106		
Vesper, The	104		
Vodka Martini	101		
Vladivostok Virgin, The	99		

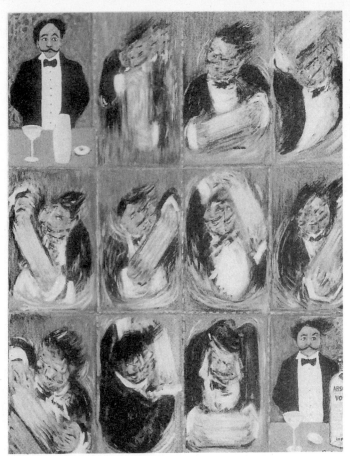

THE MARTINI MENU

FOREWORD

BY AUDREY SAUNDERS & ROBERT HESS

It's hard not to think of cocktails in general without thinking of the Martini in specific. While not the first cocktail by any stretch of the imagination, this flagship libation has spanned many thirsty generations. It was in 1997 that the first edition of *Shaken Not Stirred: A Celebration of the Martini* was published. In an era when few were taking the cocktail seriously, Jared Brown and Anistatia Miller took a decidedly different approach with this groundbreaking book, diving headlong into the exploration of the history and mythology of the Martini. Its musings were a balanced blend of information entertainment. It educated the reader with both wit and whimsy, but, more important, it revealed many long-forgotten aspects of the Martini and the people who have enjoyed them over the decades.

It is now fifteen years since its first publication, and what a change the cocktail landscape has gone through. We've seen a grand resurgence in cocktails of all types, which means we've also seen a renewed interest in the art of the Martini. Still revered as *the* quintessential cocktail, the Martini is the origin of many debates, and probably always will be. Miller

Martini is just a longer word for joy.

—Clara Bow,
silent film star

Let us candidly admit that there are shameful blemishes on the American past, of which the worst by far is rum. Nevertheless, we have improved man's lot and enriched his civilization with rye, bourbon and the martini cocktail.
In all history,
has any other nation
done so much?

—Bernard Devoto

and Brown wrote the first edition of *Shaken Not Stirred* in order to settle many of these debates, or at the very least provide well-researched context in which to take them to the next level. Over time, the arguments . . . er . . . friendly discussions surrounding the Martini have evolved, bringing new questions and new insights to bear upon the problem. It is only fitting then that this book is updated to address these issues, to add the results of new research to the discussion, and to raise new questions, as well as highlight new recipes and the people who make them.

Whether Martini novice or master, you will certainly find the pages that follow to be both enlightening and entertaining. You'll discover the ins and outs of proper Martini craftsmanship, as well as more than just a few stories to entertain your guests as you do the mixing. You'll encounter numerous recipes for drinks that are slight variations on the Martini you may be drinking now, as well as some that use this classic cocktail merely as a springboard and will help introduce you to some of the other wondrous libations that should be part of your repertoire (we would personally recommend that you check out the Fitty-Fitty and the Corpse Reviver #2 in order to see an example of both).

When we first met Jared and Anistatia, we were immediately seduced by their collective insight into all of the facets of the cocktail. They also revealed a uniquely rich view of the world and they impress with the most intricate, factual details on a myriad of topics.

As fellow colleagues, Jared and Anistatia often astound us with the breadth and depth of their research, and it's a given that we place them within an elite circle of people we consider the greatest cocktail historians in the world. Additionally, they strike us as great "cocktail detectives," with their uncanny ability to unearth historical errors within the walls of beverage history. Sherlock Holmes and Inspector Clouseau would have nothing on them.

As wonderful storytellers, they draw us in during the weeks leading up to their reveal of forthcoming liquid truths and titillate us with factual tidbits laid out like little trails of cheese to follow.

Finally, as their friends, we fall deeper in love with them with every successive discussion that we share. Over the years, our get-togethers have resulted in some of the liveliest and most thought-provoking conversations we've ever enjoyed with anyone. They are two of the most wonderful people we know and we relish every opportunity we're given to break bread or clink glasses with them.

PREFACE
& ACKNOWLEDGMENTS

Martini lovers that we are, we launched a Web site devoted entirely to Martinis on Halloween night, in 1995, called Shaken Not Stirred®: A Celebration of the Martini. A brief history as we knew it, a few classic recipes, and some lounge recommendations were our sole early offerings. Thanks to thousands of Martini aficionados worldwide (and our own slightly obsessive natures) our site grew and grew. Occasionally, we'd get a note from someone looking for a book on our favorite potable, but we hadn't found a modern volume that contained more than a half dozen recipes. (The restaurant around the corner from our Vancouver flat had sixty Martinis on its cocktail menu.)

Still, we didn't give it much thought until an editor at HarperCollins dropped us a note assuring us that there really wasn't a book that encompassed the variety of Martinis that got people to head back to cocktail lounges and hotel bars. He convinced us that we should write it. That was just the beginning.

We climbed a glacier outside Whistler in western Canada in search of clear, blue ice. We slept in the California olive groves at harvest. We made gin in Idaho, vodka in Sweden, and still make gin in London.

The Martini . . . was a drink that helped define a segment of American society . . . a more worldly, urbane sophisticate who drank in grand gin palaces fitted out with potted ferns, tile floors, brass railings, and paintings of voluptuous nudes.

—John Mariani,
America Eats Out

The perfect Martini can only be followed by another, and another and . . .

—*Playboy*,
September 1955

Anistatia standing outside in the garden with a Martini in the making: angelica on the left (used in gin) and wormwood in the foreground (which lends its name and bitterness to vermouth).

We make our own vermouth, liqueurs, and bitters from the harvests of our garden in the Cotswolds. We spend hours, months, years in the social chemistry lab, pushing the limits of white spirits, and sifting through our dog-eared personal library of lore, recipes, distillers' notes, and joke books.

Now we all know that a classic Dry Martini is made with London dry gin, as little vermouth as possible, an olive or lemon twist garnish, and nothing else. Any tradition-alists reading this book have just gotten their money's worth. However, they're welcome to join the rest of us as we read on, and enjoy some darned fine variations created over the past hundred years that also deserve to be sipped from a stemmed cocktail glass.

It's been fifteen years, a half million miles (no kidding), six changes of resi-dences (over four countries and one ocean), and a few hundred master classes in eight countries since we first took you on the first leg of our spirituous journey. We've got some old and new toasts to raise to the people who have given us advice and direction, as well as tidbits of gossip and facts that have landed in this new edition.

A round of continuing good cheer from the first edtion to Marc Nowak, Stephanie Ager Kirz, Loren "Lola" Dunsworth, the late James Kelly, Greg Connolly, Laura Baddish, and Ray Foley. Our undying gratitude has not waned toward Alison Ryley and Wayne Furman at the New York

Public Library and Debbie Randorf at the New York Historical Society Library.

A bow to Laurie Inokuma, our "Essential Japanese" translator, for instructing us in the proper way to order a Martini in the Roppongi with either an olive or a twist.

Hats off to Steve Visakay, Gerald Posner, Coreen Larson, Bob Tucker, Chris Madison, Steve Starr, Holger Faulhammer, Sean Hamilton, Ernesto Paez, Stefano Pasini, Jeffrey Carlisle, Charles Wharton, Jerry Langland, Clarke Trevett, Pete Miller, Sara Lennard, Jim Hall, and the rest of our Web friends who visited us back in those early days.

A new round of toasts go to our most loved friends Audrey Saunders and Robert Hess. May the bitters be with you. There're more that deserve huge hugs: our favorite distillers Desmond Payne and Sean Harrison; the legends Peter Dorelli, Dick Bradsell, Salvatore Calabrese, Dale DeGroff, gaz regan (aka: Gary Regan), and Alessandro Palazzi; and the upcoming legends Sasha Petraske, Nick Strangeway, Hidetsugu Ueno, Ben Reed, Angus Winchester, Henry Besant, Dré Masso, Dushan Zaric, Mauro Majoub, Douglas Ankrah, Kathy Casey, Richard Hunt, Pete Jeary, Tomas Cambral, and Paul Mant.

A rousing toast to our HarperCollins team, including our former editor, Jeremie Ruby-Strauss, who found us on the Web and drove us to drink; our present editor, Michael Signorelli, for having the chutzpah to work with us; and our wonderful copyeditor Rita Madrigal.

With that done, there's only one more thing to say: Let's party!

Cheers!

Anistatia R. Miller & Jared M. Brown

ODE
TO MY SIXTH MARTINI

Rising high above
the bar,
Your frosted stem
reveals how chilled
you are.
Clear and crisp
and dry as dust
I'll drink you now.
I will, I must.
Oh perfect gin Martini
No one shall e'er
impeach you.
Now, if only I could stand
upright,
just long enough
to reach you.

—Jared Brown

Pour servir un Cocktail

INTRODUCTION

From birth the Martini leaped to the head of the pack. In the decades when the death of the cocktail was pronounced by Jerry "the Professor" Thomas back in 1862 (in favor of the Crusta), the Martini Cocktail rose twenty years later to trump the Crusta, the Cobbler, and just about every other contender—a welcoming beacon to travelers in hotel bars, launching business lunches in steak houses, and being quietly celebrated by people who didn't give a damn if they got labeled old-fashioned or stodgy. During the early 1990s, trend-spotters predicted the return of the cocktail, a sure indicator of how far out on the trendometer it was.

Your average consumer had gained the kind of wine knowledge previously expected of a novice sommelier, and microbreweries popped up at a rate of about fifty billion a month (a rough estimate). But a little bar and restaurant in Vancouver was packing the crowds in with a sixty Martini menu. Then another place launched a Martini menu, and another and another. This trend bounced from left coast to right, from major city to city, finally fanning out into the burbs across North America.

I always remember my first Martini . . . by the third one it gets a little fuzzy.

—Jared Brown

As a young bartender I was stumped when a customer asked for a Martini. It wasn't because I didn't know what a Martini was, but because that was all he said before turning his attentions back to the captivating brunette at his elbow. Olive? Twist? Gin? Vodka? How dry? He left me dangling. After mixing her Negroni, I made a middle-of-the-road Martini for him. I watched from down the bar as he picked it up and toasted her. He sipped. He set it down. He lifted it for another sip. No reaction. Was it the best he'd had? The worst? He paid, tipped, and left. Over the years I've learned older bartenders are used to these people for whom it's just a Martini. They simply make them one to their own liking, and send them on their merry way to flummox the next young bartender.

—Jared Brown

Vintage cocktail shakers and books went from rummage sale items to become the fodder for eBay bidding frenzies. For many, a good night out was a master class in Martini mixing or at least a trip to the hot new bar to watch the bartender and soak up as much knowledge as gin. Lounge music leaped back up alongside those Martinis, and both were reshaped with the same overriding irony of a generation that could embrace this and grunge culture in the same breath.

While the more flighty aspects of the new cocktail culture have fallen away, your average cocktail drinker is far more drinks-savvy than the novice bartender of a decade ago. And bartenders—who have spent about the past six years dressed as their nineteenth-century predecessors—now embrace the true spirit of yesteryear. Not by matching the wardrobes, but by matching the professionalism and seriousness they brought to work every day. And there's no question which drink led this cocktail renaissance and continues to stand as its torch: the Martini.

But what, exactly, is a Martini? The Dry Martini is the one true Martini in much the same way that a fine bordeaux is the only red wine. You'll get about the same result in a restaurant if you simply order a Martini as if you simply request a bottle of red: Either way, you're at the mercy of the waiter or the bartender. You might end up with a house-brand California varietal table wine or an excellent 1985 Chateau Margaux. With a Martini, you might get a medium-dry, an extra-dry, or a chilled glass of gin served straight up or on the rocks.

All Martinis, in the modern context, have the same basic ancestor—mixologists call them short drinks. (Long drinks are served in tall tumblers and contain an 8:1 ratio of nonalcoholic liquid to booze.)

Professional bartending guides categorize Martinis along with their close cousin the Manhattan—a blend of whiskey and vermouth. So even in the minds of the experts, this particular cocktail branch has a fairly broad range of species and subspecies. Just like any plant, animal, or mineral on earth, you can apply scientific classification to build the Martini's family tree as we have here.

Spirits

Short Drinks
MANHATTAN | MARTINI

Long Drinks
MOJITO   ZOMBIE

MODERN MARTNI
Cosmopolitan

Modern Martinis have created an even broader definition for the "king of cocktails." Exactly what definition? You could say that a Martini is a short drink made with either gin or vodka and served straight up in a stemmed cocktail glass (aka: Martini glass). Concoctions that prescribe cognac, tequila, or whiskey as their main ingredient are definitely not members of the esteemed Martini family.

What about a Martini "on the rocks"? It's just that: a Martini served on ice. It's just like a Vodka Martini is *a* Martini, even though it's not *the* Dry Martini. But then even the Martini, historically, was not the Dry Martini. These narrow parameters are a pretty recent phenomena that developed during the postwar 1940s and 1950s when upper-level executives dictated America's—and the world's—tastes.

A Latin scholar from Cambridge walked into The Mill Pub, took a seat at the bar, and called to the owner, "Give me a Martinus, please."

"You mean Martini, sir?" the owner inquired as he set up a shaker.

The scholar hastily answered, "If I want more than one I'll tell you."

It's never too early for a cocktail.

—Noël Coward,
The Vortex (1926)

We've uncovered more than a hundred Martini recipes that were created between the 1890s and 1930s. Variations are not a new trend, they're a rediscovery of worldly individualism.

Finally, we pondered one more serious question that befalls every serious Martini drinker: When's the best time to drink one? In Ernest Hemingway's *Islands in the Stream*, it never seemed to be too early or too late:

> ...[Thomas Hudson] looked at his watch. "Why don't we just have a quick one?"
>
> "Fine. I could use one." [Roger replied]
>
> "It isn't quite twelve."
>
> "I don't think that makes any difference. You're through working and I'm on vacation. But maybe we better wait until twelve if that's your rule."
>
> "All right."
>
> "I've been keeping that rule, too. It's an awful nuisance some mornings when a drink would make you feel alright."
>
> "Let's break it," Thomas Hudson said. "I get awfully excited when I know I'm going to see them," he explained.
>
> "I know."
>
> "Joe," Roger called. "Bring the shaker and rig for Martinis."
>
> "Yes, sir. I got her rigged now."
>
> "What did you rig so early for? Do you think we're rummies!"
>
> "No sir. Mr. Roger. I figured that was what you were saving that empty stomach for."

SHAKEN NOT STIRRED

MARTINI ZEN

THE ART OF FINE MIXOLOGY

So you already know how to make a darn good Martini. Frankly, that's not good enough. You want to make the best Martini that ever graced the inner curve of a thoroughly chilled long-stemmed cocktail glass. You don't just want a Perfect Martini (*see page 80*); you want Martini perfection! No? It's your first time, and you just want your date—who's arriving for cocktails in ten minutes—to believe that you've made a Martini before? Either way, read on!

The first thing to realize is that there are very few components to a Martini. There are the ingredients: gin (or vodka), vermouth (or its replacement), ice, and garnish. Then there's the equipment: a cocktail shaker or mixing glass and stirring spoon, long-stemmed glasses, and swizzle sticks or toothpicks. That's it. So it's through the proper manipulation and balance of these few items that you're going to produce liquid satin instead of a drink that'll leave you licking stamps just to get the taste out of your mouth. This, young Grasshopper, is Martini Zen.

NORA CHARLES:
How many drinks have you had?
NICK CHARLES:
This will make six Martinis.
NORA CHARLES:
[to the waiter] All right. Will you bring me five more Martinis, Leo? Line them right up here.
— *The Thin Man* (1934)

NICK CHARLES:
See, in mixing, the important thing is the rhythm. Always have rhythm in your shaking. Now a Manhattan, you shake to fox trot time; a Bronx to two-step time. But a Martini, you always shake to waltz time.
— *The Thin Man* (1934)

The one who drives
When he's been drinking
Depends on you
To do his thinking.

—Burma Shave roadside
sign from the 1930s

EIGHT COMMANDMENTS
OF MARTINI MAKING & DRINKING

If you aspire to being a master Martini mixologist there are eight commandments to which to you must adhere as both participant and responsible host—the guardian of your guests' health and happiness:

Commandment No. 1: Do use the finest ingredients you can afford. Mixers like soda, tonic, or juice can hide a multitude of sins, especially when they comprise the majority of a drink. But in a Martini, that's not the case. This cocktail depends on the quality of its few ingredients for its flavor. Since most of that is the liquor, if it's no good, neither is the drink.

Commandment No. 2: Don't encourage drinking games. Save group entertainment for lower-proof drinks like gin and tonics or beer. It's like going four-wheeling in a limited-edition Range Rover. Sure, it'd be fun—but what a waste. You may not need a permit to carry one, but a Martini is not a toy.

Commandment No. 3: Don't use aluminum mixing implements. To quote one visitor to our Web site, "Bleeeeeccchh!" Aluminum degrades quickly when it comes in contact with acids (like lemon oil or juice). When it does, this metal imparts its unique essence into the mix: a liquid version of nibbling the wrapper off a Hershey's Kiss. Likewise, copper and, some say, silver have the same effect. (Although we suspect the latter might just be the tarnish cleaning off into your drink.) Stick to glass or stainless steel implements—the strongest flavor in your drink should be the drink itself.

Commandment No. 4: Don't perform certain physical activities. Anybody can remind you and your guests not to drink and drive. We completely agree (don't drink and drive), but we'd like to add a few other cautionary notes. Please *don't* drink Martinis and Rollerblade; snowboard; ski (either downhill, cross-country, or ski jump); handle unsheathed Samurai swords; play darts blindfolded; walk the tightrope wearing hockey skates; wrestle alligators; gnaw on electrical cords; play with lawn darts; swim; complete your federal tax return; play the French horn; walk barefoot on hot coals; monopolize the karaoke microphone; or anything else that goes against your sober common sense.

You know your Martini is too watered down when . . .

If you find all this a bit restrictive, you'll be glad to know that there is one activity that requires copious Martini consumption *before you begin.* Take a vacation in the Philippines and join the locals hunting for venomous sea snakes. Before they enter the coral reefs, divers drink up a storm to fortify themselves while they work. According to them, if you have enough alcohol in your bloodstream, it protects you from the sea snake's deadly bite.

Commandment No. 5: Don't have too much or too little dilution. You've got a brand-new shaker loaded up, you've got Groove Armada on the stereo, and you're shaking like a fool. By the time you're done shakin' that drink to "I See You Baby," your Martini's life is over. On the other hand, pouring gin straight from the freezer into the glass and then forming a mental picture of a vermouth bottle is about the same as swigging directly from the bottle. Dilution is as essential to the drink as the chill.

The first drink I made for a customer was a Negroni, a close cousin to the Martini. The bartender who trained me (for about twenty minutes) said, "If you don't know the drink, smile! Say, 'Ah, that's a great drink but I haven't made it in a while. Let me check the proportions.' Then grab the Mr. Boston and look it up." And so I did. Any other night I'd have been mortified to see the proportions were one part gin to one part vermouth to one part Campari. That night I was just glad Negroni didn't turn out to be a brand of Italian beer.

—Jared Brown

Commandment No. 6: Don't use gigantic glassware. Every shop sells them bigger and taller than the last place. These aren't Martini glasses, they're nacho bowls, birdbaths. Do you really want to drink out of something Dita Von Teese uses to perform her burlesque act? (Don't answer that.) Two small, perfectly chilled Martinis are better than one behemoth that you'll never see the bottom of before it rises to the temperature of the hand holding the glass. That works for brandy, and this is not brandy.

Commandment No. 7: Don't pour your drink into a warm glass. You keep your gin in the freezer. Your ice is rock hard and chilled far below freezing. You stir until the mixing glass leaves you with frostbitten fingertips. Then, with a flourish, you strain that honey-thick Martini into a piping hot glass fresh from the dishwasher. Here, the second law of thermodynamics steps in, and all the heat energy jumps from the glass into your drink.

Commandment No. 8: Don't rely too much on the experts. Yes, there are people out there who have calculated the mass and volume of an average drop of orange bitters and insist on using an insulin syringe with the needle removed to administer the precise amount into the shaker (our apologies to the significant other of any Martini fanatic who hadn't already thought of that one). Not to mention how many square millimeters of lemon twist you need.

These experts may tell you it's the only way to make a palatable Martini and treat your best efforts like a mother admiring her baby's first mudpie. Let them mix their own. You know when you've got yours right because it tastes right to you. And when you reach that point, the ultimate in suave and debonair is doing away with the props and the preaching and mixing them offhandedly without losing track of the conversation like you've mixed a million. And smile. You're about to have a great Martini.

After cutting twists, wash the knife immediately. The acid in the lemon dissolves the micro-thin knife edge, dulling it in minutes. Any chef will tell you that a sharp knife is safer (less likely to slip off whatever you're cutting) than a dull knife.

A PRIMER ON TERMS & MEASURES

Until you get used to counting or eyeballing your measurements like a pro, it doesn't hurt to have a shot glass with indications for 1 oz. (30 ml) and 0.5 oz. (15 ml) printed or etched on the side, a teaspoon, and a tablespoon in your bar equipment inventory. There are also a few bar terms you should learn to recognize:

1 dash	0.125 teaspoon (5 ml)
1 splash	0.25 oz. (10 ml)
1 tablespoon (1 tbsp.)	0.5 oz. (15 ml)
1 pony	1 oz. (30 ml)
1 jigger or shot	1.5 oz. (45 ml)
a twist	strip of lemon peel
light Martini	2 oz. Martini
regular (standard) Martini	3 oz. Martini
large (boardroom) Martini	4 oz. Martini
double (Chicago) Martini	8 oz. Martini*
straight up, up, or chilled neat	served without ice
on the rocks	served with ice

* Save the toothpick. Use it to dial AA.

POURING LIKE A PRO

Did you ever see the 1988 movie *Cock-tail*? Yes? Did you go home and make a total mess of your kitchen like the rest of us? Okay, so those shakers were glued shut, the bottles were sealed, and who knows how many retakes they actually did to get those bottle-tossing, drink-flinging flair bartending scenes right. But the actors couldn't fake those perfect pours. With a little practice, you can pour just as accurately.

First, go buy a couple of those nifty tops they use on liquor bottles in bars. (Most kitchen equipment stores have them. They're called speed pourers.) Go home, fill an empty liquor bottle with water, and stick a speed pourer on it. Grasp the bottle by the neck and turn it completely upside down over a shot glass. Count to four (or five if you prefer) in the time it takes to pour a 1.5 oz. shot. Next, try pouring to the same count into a regular glass. Empty the contents into the shot glass to see how closely you measured. Figure it should take about a hundred pours to master this skill. (That's why you've got to use water.) From there you can easily enhance your repertoire by pouring a splash (a one count), a dash (cover the little opening with your thumb and pour a one count), and a drop (cover the big opening with your thumb and pour a one count).

MASTERFUL MIXING

The late, great James Kelly, head bartender at the Four Seasons Restaurant in New York—and one of the world's best mixologists—demonstrated his Martini-making method for us. After filling a glass shaker with gin and vermouth, he then stirred the mixture rapidly for precisely twenty-one seconds. Although he never glanced at his watch, we secretly timed him as he repeated the process for each of three Martinis. Maybe our ability to read our watches slipped a little, but his timing didn't falter by a second.

The first rule of shaking is to make sure the lid's on tight. (Do this every time. Unlike pasta, you can't tell if a Martini's done by tossing it against the wall to see if it sticks.) Then hold the shaker at a slight angle and shake gently with an up-and-down motion. Vigorous shaking throws a lot more ice shards into the mix.

PROTECTING THE FLAVOR

You may have gallons of the best vodka or gin and premium vermouth, but if you haven't touched those freezer-flavored ice trays since you moved into your house, you've ruined your Martini before you've begun. Ask yourself these pertinent questions before pouring those precious liquids over the cubes:

- Did you wash the trays before you made the ice?
- Is the ice fresh? Or is it encrusted with the frosty remnants of last year's chili-fest?
- How's the water? If the tap water you use to make the ice tastes funny, so will the Martini, unless you use bottled water.
- If that doesn't seem to work, a box of baking soda in the freezer might be the cure.
- To really impress or baffle your friends, you can add all sorts of things to the ice (no plastic bugs, please). Some of our favorites are a dash of vermouth or Cointreau, flower petals, or a splash of cranberry juice cocktail.

The original Silver Bullet. Gossip writer Earl Wilson, best known for his syndicated "It Happened Last Night" column, fired the first icy shot on February 18, 1972, when he introduced America to the "Silver Bullet Recipe– Martini With Scotch." He discovered it in Pittsburgh's West Bar, where he'd ordered a Gibson on the rocks with a float of Pernod. The bartender was out of Pernod and offered him a Silver Bullet instead. When Earl asked the obvious question, "What's a Silver Bullet?" the bartender replied, "A Martini with some scotch floating on top. We've been making them that way for years."

When Earl introduced the drink to legendary New York imbiber Toots Shor, he said, "A Martini with scotch? I can't wait till I tell Jackie Gleason!"

CONTROLLING THE STRENGTH

Other than the obvious (more or less booze), it's easy to make a Martini stronger or more user friendly. Here are a few tips:

- Crushed or cracked ice melts faster than cubes, adding more water to the mix when it's shaken.

- Room-temperature liquor instead of freezer-chilled has the same effect: It melts the ice faster.

- The longer you shake the mix, the more the ice melts.

- Using freezer-chilled vodka or gin and mixing without ice makes a stronger drink, but keep in mind that the right amount of dilution really helps the flavor.

THE QUALITY OF THE GARNISH

High-quality olives or a fresh lemon twist are the perfect finish to the perfectly produced Martini. If you want the ultimate olive garnish, you can either marinate oversize olives in vermouth, or you can hunt around for "tipsy olives" or "tipsy onions," which are packed in vermouth rather than regular brine. There are also olives stuffed with garlic, anchovies, blue cheese, almonds, even jalapeño peppers. There are two methods for cutting twists. Jared learned one at his first bartending job: a place that used $2.49 bottles of American "champagne" for their Mimosas. He was taught to cut the ends off the lemon, loosen the insides with a full twist of the bar spoon and push them out (easier than it sounds), and cut the resulting empty barrel in half lengthwise and then cross-wise into twist strips. Voilà, uniform twists and minimal waste.

He picked up the second method at the Rainbow Room in Manhattan while watching the service bartender set up for the lunch shift. He took only the freshest lemons, washed them gently, and pared as many large ovals of peel off the outside as he could by slicing the lemon from top to bottom, unconcerned that he wasn't getting 100 percent of the fruit. As a result, his twists were shaped like mini potato chips, with mostly yellow peel and only the slightest bit of white underneath.

The ideal tool for cutting twists without paring your fingertips is a vegetable peeler.

SERVING WITH STYLE

A big part of the Martini experience is the presentation: a perfectly clean, chilled Martini glass, a frosty shaker, the sound of the ice shifting inside it as the drink is poured slowly. This is what the cocktail is all about.

One final note. If you want to pre-batch Martinis before a party, you can combine the gin and vermouth—and bitters if you like them—but do not add the ice. It's like pulling the pin on a grenade. Batch your drinks into clean glass bottles. (We use clip-top bottles like the ones that Grolsch beer uses.)

From that point on you have to count the seconds and get it back off the ice before all is lost.

Perfect twists and other garnishes can be cut ahead of time, but not days ahead of time. The difference in appearance and taste between a fresh-cut and days-old lemon twist or wedge, especially in warmer climates, is the difference between garnish and compost.

Now, you're ready to embark on your own road to Martini nirvana. We can't offer advice on which recipe to try first or last. That is a personal choice, one that each aficionado must make on his or her own. Be prepared for all sorts of advice—which reminds us of a story Bob Tucker, an entrant in our 1996 Shaken Not Stirred® Martini Story Competition, sent us:

> The entire Royal Canadian Mounted Police carry a small survival kit with them at all times in a small leather, zippered case. Inside, there are miniature bottles of gin and vermouth. The kit also contains a small metal cup, a swizzle stick, and a card that instructs the Mountie: Should he/she become hopelessly lost in the wilderness, they should sit down, take out the survival kit, and begin making a Martini. Before the drink is mixed it's guaranteed someone will appear to rescue them, saying, "No, no, that's not the way to make a Martini!"

½ - GIN-DRY
½ - GRAPE FRUIT JUICE
DASH GRENADINE

MAMIE

MARTINI

MANHATTAN

1 DASH
BITTERS ANGOSTURA
5/8 - GIN-DRY
¼ - VERMOUTH DRY
⅛ - VERMOUTH ITALIAN

1 DASH
BITTERS ANGOSTURA
2 DASHES
MARASCHINO
½ - RYE
½ - VERMOUTH ITALIAN

CRAC
1 PO
S
FILL
GIN
MAR
SER

2 DASHES
ORANGE BITTERS
2 DASHES
BITTERS ANGOSTURA
⅔ - BRANDY
2 DASHES
GUM SYRUP
⅓ - VERMOUTH DRY

BERMUDA

BETWEEN SHEETS

OM
ONS
WINEGLASS
OF WATER
TSPN GR. SUGAR
DECORATE
WITH MINT & FRUIT

BOULEVARDE

⅓ BRANDY
⅓ GIN-DRY
⅓ CURACAO

1 DASH
LEMON JUICE

¼ APRICO
½ - GIN
¼ GR

3
LEM
1
GR

2/5 GIN-DRY
⅕ ORANGE J'CE
⅕ VERMOUTH DRY
⅕ VERMOUTH ITALIAN

HA P

RY GIN
GE JUICE
MOUTH

CHAPTER ONE

TOP SHELF

THE RISE & REFINEMENT OF THE CLASSIC MARTINI

More intellectual duels have been waged over the Martini's origins than for any other cocktail (and just as many feuds over its preparation have parted close allies). However, there is a détente. All factions mutually agree, Martinis must be made and presented with style. Traditions die hard, and we're grateful that this singular golden rule is the point of difference between the drink known as the "elixir of quietude" and other alcoholic beverages, like shooters, coolers, umbrella drinks, and Jell-O shots.

As in any rite of passage, neophytes must prepare for the initiation that takes them from the adolescent world of keg parties to the refinement of the Martini. Elders of this growing sect are well versed in the enigmatic questions of mixology; they faithfully practice the prescribed rituals both in public and private. They revere the drink's champions. They tell tales that have been passed down from generation to generation about the Martini's origins and its rise to elegance. They share the names and locations of sophisticated Martini shrines they've discovered along the way.

THE TOP TEN ALLEGED MARTINI INVENTORS

1. J.P.A. Martini, Paris, France, circa 1763

2. Parker's Saloon, Boston, MA, 1850

3. Jerry Thomas, Martinez, CA, 1852 (or San Francisco, CA, 1860)

4. Harry Johnson, San Francisco, CA, 1860

5. Heublein Company, Hartford, CT, 1894

6. Martini & Rossi, Turin, Italy, 1890

7. The American Bar at the Savoy, London, UK, 1910

8. Signor Martinez, Waldorf-Astoria Hotel, New York, NY, 1910

9. Martini di Arma di Taggia, Knickerbocker Hotel, New York, NY, 1910

10. Harry MacElhone, The New York Bar, Paris, France, 1911

A

Compleat Body

OF

DISTILLING,

Explaining the

MYSTERIES

OF THAT

SCIENCE,

IN

A most easy and familiar Manner;

Containing an

Exact and Accurate Method of making all the
COMPOUND CORDIAL-WATERS now in Use;

WITH

A particular Account of their several Virtues.

As also a

DIRECTORY

Consisting of

All the INSTRUCTIONS necessary for learning the
DISTILLER'S ART; with a Computation of
the original Cost of the several Ingredients, and the
Profits arising in Sale.

Adapted no less to the Use of private Families, than of
APOTHECARIES and DISTILLERS.

IN TWO PARTS.

By GEORGE SMITH, of *Kendall* in *Westmorland*.

The THIRD EDITION.

LONDON:

Printed for HENRY LINTOT, at the *Cross Keys* against
St. *Dunstan's* Church in *Fleetstreet*. MDCCXXXVIII.

GIN & SIN
CLASSIC GIN MARTINIS

Armagnac and eau-de-vie were the first to be adopted as pleasurable libations, during the 1300s, after Arnaud de Villeneuve discovered the secret of making aqua vitae (aka: water of life). But we are far more interested in the work of Belgian physician Philippus Hermanni, who, in 1552, recorded the recipe for making a malted grain eau-de-vie, called *eau-de-genever* (aka: juniper water).

We only have to pop next door to the Netherlands to meet the person who received the most notoriety for his distillation skills. Thanks to successful colonies in Asia, the Americas, and Africa, Dutch chemists and distillers had a veritable cornucopia of exotic ingredients at their fingertips. University of Leyden professor Dr. Sylvius de Bouve capitalized on this bounty, in 1565, creating a kidney tonic and lumbago remedy by rectifying a grain spirit with juniper berries. Word got around about this medical marvel and its pleasant pine aroma. Not that the locals were suffering from an epidemic of kidney problems and back pains. They liked sipping what was now dubbed genever simply for pleasure.

I'm tired of gin,
I'm tired of sin,
And after last night,
Oh boy, am I tired.

—Anonymous

Some great English dry gins to try include: Beefeater, Beefeater 24, No. 3, Oxley, Plymouth, Plymouth Navy Strength, Sacred, Sipsmith, Tanqueray, Tanqueray No. Ten.

Not in the realm of the classic dry style, but one of the best new-style gins to try is Hendrick's.

When King William of Orange, England's only Dutch king, returned to his home country for a visit, he brought his physician, who wrote a truly mind-numbing book describing the gardens in the king's Dutch palace (perhaps it is a ripping read to the multitudes of ornamental garden historians out there).

However, he devoted one chapter to the food and drink he encountered in Holland. And what were they drinking? Not once was genever mentioned.

This is not surprising. It was a medicinal, and considering the state of distillation back then, it probably tasted pretty medicinal. No, in the cafés, the royal sawbones noted, they were drinking French white wine infused with wormwood; basically, they were sitting in the midst of the birth of gin, palates drenched in vermouth. No record yet as to whether some local barkeep was mixing the two.

Despite all the British government's attempts to control—or quash—gin production in the eighteenth century, the solution came not from regulating gin but deregulating beer. When Prime Minister Arthur Wellesley, the Duke of Wellington, passed the Beer Act of 1830, which dropped the tax on beer and cider, England became a nation of beer drinkers overnight. This caused the lesser distilleries to fail, leaving only the best gin for the most discerning customers.

Soon after, around two hundred distilleries popped up around the Netherlands to meet a growing demand. The "het Lootsje" distillery owned by Jacobus Bols became especially successful with this venture when, in 1602, it was commissioned to supply the Dutch East India Company with spirits and liqueurs. In 1664, the order included genever: A daily ration of a half pint was issued to both the company's officers and crew.

The British love affair with this aromatic spirit began when Britons came to the aid of the Dutch, defeating the Spanish during the Dutch Revolt (1567–1609). Their daily ration of genever, issued prior to battle, gave them "Dutch courage." It's no wonder that they were more than happy to come to the Netherlands' aid once again during the Thirty Years' War (1618–1648), since it meant they could drink more genever.

We must tip our hats to Britain's only Dutch monarch, William of Orange, who encouraged genever consumption when he ascended the throne in 1689. He not only made it fashionable at court, he promoted the importation of genever and distillation of British gin from the bumper-crop grain harvest.

Londoners fully embraced this royal decree. Daniel Defoe, author of *Robinson*

Crusoe, lauded good William, writing in 1713, "Nothing is more certain than the fact that the ordinary production of grain in England is much greater than our people or cattle can consume. Because gin is made from grain, the distilling trade is one remedy for this disaster as it helps to carry off the great quantity of grain in such a time of plenty. In times of plenty and a moderate price of grain, the distilling of grain is one of the most essential things to support the landed interest and therefore especially to be preserved."

Distilleries popped up like posies. With tax-free production, gin was cheaper to produce than beer and thus cheaper to drink. Seemingly overnight, gin—both good and downright horrible—flowed through London like the waters of the River Thames. The 1721 Excise Revenue Accounts recorded that one out of every four habitable structures in the British capital distilled some form of gin. Nearly 7,000 gin shops served two million gallons of tax-free gin to London's growing population of 500,000 men, women, and children.

Fortunately, this "Gin Craze" and the production of poor-quality gin was suppressed by the late 1790s through the separate licensing of spirit distillation and gin rectification as well as heavy taxation on distillates. Yet the taste for gin never diminished, it just reached a quality-conscious audience who could afford to buy it.

Thomas Coates of the Black Friars Distillery in Plymouth, Devon, in 1793, developed the world's first dry-style gin. When Britain went to war with Napoléon Bonaparte, in 1803, Royal Navy admiral Lord Horatio Nelson ordered barrels of Coates's gin to supply his officers with their daily ration.

The only gin to be awarded a Geographical Designation from the European Union, Plymouth dry gin macerates juniper berries, angelica root, cardamom, coriander, orris root, and lemon and orange peels into grain spirit.

In addition to juniper berries, London dry gins are made with a variety of botanicals, including angelica root and seeds, orris root, lemon peel, orange peel, calamus, coriander, bitter almonds, caraway, cassia, and licorice.

Coates was not the only master distiller to garner such overwhelming commercial success. London rectifiers James Lys Seager, William Evans, Alexander Gordon, Walter and Alfred Gilbey, Charles Tanqueray, Sir Robert Burnett, as well as John and Willam Nicholson produced an even drier style—the London dry gin style.

Another London distiller managed to literally put his name on the map. Sir Felix Booth achieved fame with his London dry gin and shared some of his fortune, in 1829, when he contributed £17,000 to James Ross's arctic circle expedition to find the Northwest Passage. The explorer thanked his benefactor by naming the Boothia Felix Peninsula—the Canadian Northwest Territories' northernmost tip—after him.

These new styles of dry gin were the featured offerings at London drinking establishments such as Thompson & Fearon's and Weller's, which were soon followed by Princess Louise, Princess Victoria, and other "gin palaces." Garishly decorated and brightly lit, the gin palace was a gathering place that offered respite from the sometimes bleak world of nineteenth-century London. Author Charles Dickens heartily approved of these new watering holes. In his 1836 collection of stories, *Sketches by Boz,* he wrote:

All is light and brilliancy. The hum of many voices issues from the splendid gin-shop which forms the commencement of the two streets opposite; and the gay building with the fantastically ornamented parapet, the illuminated lock, the plate-glass windows surrounded by stucco rosettes and its profusion of gas-lights in richly-gilt burners, is perfectly dazzling when contrasted with the darkness and dirt we have just left.

By the time Queen Victoria ascended to the British throne, in 1837, gin distillers had perfected nearly seven distinct styles. In addition to the the floral Plymouth style and the citrusy London style, Dr. Sheridan Muspratt recorded recipes for two types of cordial gin, fine gin, West Country gin, plain gin, geneva, and plain geneva culled from interviews with Britain's leading gin distilleries.

Gone were the days of the Gin Craze, cheap gin that smelled like turpentine, and the unemployed who guzzled shots for a penny a piece. Dry Gin was the daily ration of Royal Navy officers and the afternoon tipple of elegant society ladies who sipped the spirit out of teacups.

As gin achieved both quality and sophistication, it also stepped into the limelight as the feature spirit in a new mixed drink—the cocktail.

The word "proof" originates from a simple test to measure the alcohol content in spirits by pouring the liquor onto gunpowder and igniting it. If the powder burned, it indicated that there was sufficient alcohol—or proof. This was deemed 100 proof, though it is actually around 57 percent ABV.

This test replaced less accurate measures such as igniting a piece of cloth soaked in spirit to see if the spirit would burn cleanly away without harming the cloth, or simply attempting to ignite the spirit. During the Napoleonic Wars, Thomas Coates developed Plymouth Navy Strength, a 57 percent ABV gin that was strong enough to pass the Royal Navy's "proof" test.

COCK-TAIL

VULGARLY CALLED "GINGER"

Stir

2 oz. (60 ml) gin

0.5 oz. (15 ml) curaçao

0.5 oz. (15 ml) fresh ginger syrup

2 dashes Angostura bitters

Moisten the rim of a rocks glass with lemon juice. Build ingredients in the glass. Stir and add rock ice.

. . . and began to dose [the horse] with a pint of gin and ginger twice a day. The stimulant kept up the spirits of the animal so that he worked all the time, and in less than a week earned one hundred and ninety-two dollars. Unfortunately, however, the horse has acquired a taste for intoxicating liquor, and cannot do without it now. He smells it as he passes saloons, and insists upon stopping; neither will he eat his food unless it is thus seasoned.

—*Ballou's Monthly Magazine*, volume 37 (January–June 1873)

The Internet is a wonderful thing. You can scan the day's current events over a morning cup of coffee or you can seek solace, like we do, rummaging through old newspaper and magazine archives with a click of the mouse. Not that we don't have enough reading material in the house with our personal library of more than a thousand vintage cocktail and distillation books. We just like a little light reading before we start the day's excavations.

One morning, while we were researching our two-volume tome *Spirituous Journey: A History of Drink,* we fell upon a real eye opener.

We're sure that if you've been following the past decade's cocktail renaissance at all you know the word "cocktail" was first defined in print in the May 13, 1806, edition of *The Balance, and Columbian Repository* newspaper of Hudson, New York: "a stimulating liquor, composed of spirits of any kind, sugar, water and bitters it is vulgarly called a bittered sling . . ." The editor Harry Croswell scribed this annotation after a reader questioned its meaning in a satirical piece that had been published the week before.

But on that brisk morning, we found an earlier reference to the term that gave us even more to ponder. This cocktail appeared in London. Not just London. It sprouted up in the heart of London politics: Downing Street, at the Axe & Gate Public House on the corner of Downing and Whitehall. Yes, politics (or at least politicians) have been soaked in cocktails since the birth of the word.

On March 16, 1798, the *Morning Post and Gazetteer* reported that a pub owner won a lottery and erased all his customers' debts: "A publican, in Downing-street, who had a share of the 20,000 l. prize, rubbed out all his scores, in a transport of joy: This was a humble imitation of his neighbour who, when he drew the highest prize in the state lottery, not only rubbed out, but actually broke scores with his old customers, and entirely forgot them."

The next week, the March 20, 1798, edition satirically listed details of seventeen politicians' pub debts, documenting who owed for what including the following:

> Mr. Pitt,
> two petit vers of "L'huile de Venus"
> Ditto, one of "perfeit amour"
> Ditto, "cock-tail"
> (vulgarly called ginger)

Mr. Pitt—William Pitt the Younger—was Britain's premier (aka: prime minister) when this article appeared. His tenure was marked by the French Revolution and the Napoleonic Wars. So that explains the French drinks he purportedly put on his tab.

But why was his cocktail "vulgarly called ginger"? Then again, why was Croswell's cocktail "vulgarly called a bittered sling" eight years later?

We leaped into the library and dug out the first British drinks book to include cocktails, William Terrington's 1869 *Cooling Cups and Dainty Drinks*. Low and behold, his Gin Cocktail contained a healthy dose of ginger syrup!

If, by definition, a cocktail is a drink with spirits, sugar, water, and bitters, is a Martini a cocktail? According to a couple of pre-Prohibition mandarins of mixing it is, as the bitters and touch of sweetness come from the vermouth, the dilution comes from the ice, and everything else comes from the gin.

The one amazing thing about our vernacular is that we know less of the origin of comparatively modern terms that we use than we do about words that have formed part of our tongue for centuries. Legend has played with cocktail just as it did with cockney, and if we wish to be candid with ourselves, all that we can do is acknowledge the fact that their origin is unknown. The first cocktail had ginger as one of its ingredients. It serves as a bracer, and helped to "pep up" those who took it.

—from the article "The Romance of Words," Dr. Frank B. Vizetelly, managing editor, Funk & Wagnalls *New Standard Dictionary of the English Language* (August 19, 1929)

Okay. That could have been a one-off usage of the word. But then as we were writing this edition of *Shaken Not Stirred®*, we fell upon a September 21, 1924, article in *The New York Times* that mentions Dr. Frank Horace Vizetelly's quest to find the origin of the word "cocktail."

In his 1923 book *The Desk-Book of Idioms and Idiomatic Phrases in English Speech and Literature,* he had traced the term to Washington Irving's *A Knickerbocker's History of New York.* (Been there. Done that.) But in the article it was noted: "While Dr. Vizetelly said he could add nothing officially to this definition and history of the cocktail, he was inclined to think that the term was in some way traceable to the horse referred to in old English and old Irish chronicles as 'a cock-tail.'"

Vizetelly discovered "it was the custom of trainers and horsemen before exhibiting animals of this kind to give them a dose of ginger mixed with water or other invigorating concoction in order to stimulate their antics in the show ring."

The reporter added, "It is not unlikely, according to Dr. Vizetelly, that an aromatic mixture for general consumption grew out of this custom."

Before the night was out we found a refreshment called Gin & Gingerbread from 1731 and Victorian references to giving horses gin and ginger. If only we could contact Vizetelly in the great beyond to show him our 1798 find. He could have rewritten a portion of cocktail history during the dry depths of Prohibition.

This is not the end of our story about the Martini's ancestor, the Gin Cocktail. However, first we need to take you on a slight detour to talk about another gin drink that got British hearts a-fluttering.

PINK GIN

ATTRIBUTED TO DON CARLOS SIEGERT

Cocktails and bitters. The two seemed an ideal pair back in those early days. The first commercially produced and patented aromatic bitter was created by a south London apothecarist named Richard Stoughton. Containing twenty-two ingredients, his Elixir Magnum Stomachii received Britain's second government-issued patent for a compound medicine in 1712. The dosage was generous: fifty to sixty drops "in a glass of Spring water, Beer, Ale, Mum, Canary, White wine, with or without sugar, and a dram of brandy as often as you please."

The true market for this miracle of modern medicine were ladies and gentlemen who relished its piquant character, sipping small shots for pleasure. Exported to the colonies by the barrel loads until the American Revolution of 1776, citizens of the new nation discovered freedom had a price. They could no longer import Stoughton's bitters. This prompted the launch of stateside manufacturers who eagerly supplied despondent Americans' demand for bitters. One producer was Antoine Amédée Peychaud, who created an aromatic bitters that he introduced to the citizens of New Orleans in samples mixed with brandy and sugar that he dispensed in his apothecary on Rue Royale.

The call for aromatic bitters also triggered the career of Dr. Johann Gottlieb Benjamin Siegert, who, while working as surgeon general for Simon Bolivar's revolutionary army in Venezuela, developed a digestive bitters to aid troops suffering

Let stand

1 oz. (30 ml) Plymouth gin

1 oz. (30 ml) still water

2 dashes Angostura bitters

Coat the glass with bitters. Then add the gin until the liquid turns pink. Finish with water.

The 1895 recipe for the **Plymouth Cocktail** shook 1.5 oz. (45 ml) Plymouth gin and 3 dashes orange bitters, garnished with a lemon peel or a maraschino cherry.

SINCE 1793

We give lots of seminars on cocktails. These are normally fun affairs. One afternoon, in New Orleans, everyone seemed to be in the spirit except an unsmiling gent at a table near the front. So, after demonstrating the classic way to make a Pink Gin, I walked it over and said, "This one's for you, sir." He looked shocked, but not half as shocked as I was after the seminar when he said to me, "In Vietnam, I brought every member of my company home alive, except one. I mixed them all a daily Pink Gin, but one of my men didn't drink. He died of malaria. I thought no one mixed Pink Gin anymore. Thank you."

from "jungle belly"—Amargo Aromatico. This remedy worked so well that Siegert changed careers, establishing a distillery in 1830 located in Angostura (now called Ciudad Bolívar) to supply demand.

At the 1862 Great London Exposition, locals were introduced to hordes of imported inventions and advances. Don Carlos Siegert exhibited his father's digestive bitters, which he renamed Angostura bitters. A savvy marketer, the young Siegert paid close attention to all the ruckus about cocktails before unveiling his presentation: He passed out samples of bitters mixed with gin and a splash of water. Legend has it that a Royal Navy ship's surgeon then used the concoction to combat seamen's stomach complaints and fatigue. Naval officers called it Pinkers. Londoners called it Pink Gin.

Pinkers remained a beloved British tipple despite the changing fads and fancies that followed. It even fortified the spirit of a great adventurer. A recent cancer survivor, aviator and sailor Sir Francis Charles Chichester sipped a daily ration of Pink Gin while he sailed alone around the world, in 1966, onboard his 53-foot yacht the *Gipsy Moth IV*. If you spent 107 days sailing nonstop from Plymouth, England, to Sydney, Australia, you'd certainly need fortification. Chichester tackled the 119-day return trip savoring the same sip. When he returned to Plymouth, he explained to reporters and a cheering crowd that the darkest day of his voyage was the day the gin ran out.

Were the Cock-tail (vulgarly called "ginger") and Pink Gin the Martini's respectable ancestors? We pondered these primal origins as we crossed the English Channel to investigate a French source.

MARTINI'S MARTINI

ATTRIBUTED TO JEAN-PAUL AEGIDE MARTINI

Our heartfelt thanks to *American Heritage* magazine for citing us for this, "the most far-fetched birth of the Martini." Keep half-reading, guys.

Johann Paul Aegius Schwarzendorf is the Martini's only alleged (and not alleged by us!) inventor who was not a bartender or beverage company. Born in Freistadt, Germany, on September 1, 1741, Schwarzendorf was a musical prodigy by the age of ten when he was awarded a post as the organist in a Jesuit seminary. His biographers reported that young Johann went home around 1758 to find a wicked stepmother installed at his family abode. Not amused by this change of events, the musician packed his belongings lock, stock, and barrel, traveling to Nancy, France, in search of fame and fortune even though he didn't speak the language and didn't have a penny to his name. Schwarzendorf was befriended by a local organ builder named Dupont who advised him to change his name to Jean-Paul Aegide Martini. (Italian composers were all the rage in those days.) Three years later, Martini took the fast lane to glory, receiving the coveted position of court composer for King Stanislaw I of Poland, Duke of Lorraine, who was living at Lunéville, France.

His mentor died in 1766, but once again Lady Luck favored Martini, who became the toast of Paris society by winning a heated competition to write a march for the Swiss Guard. He followed that success by scribing a number of popular light operas, a cantata written expressly for Emperor Napoléon's wedding ceremony,

Let stand

2 oz. (60 ml) *genièvre*

1 oz. (30 ml) Rhine wine or Chablis

1 pinch ground cinnamon

A few varieties of dry white wine to try include: Pouilly-Fuissé, Bordeaux Blanc, Fumé Blanc, and Sauvignon Blanc.

Good thing Martini changed his name. Can you imagine saying: "Hey, bartender. Could we get another round of extra-dry Schwarzendorfs?" So much for the three-Martini lunch, no one would have been able to say it after two drinks.

The three-Martini lunch is the epitome of American efficiency. Where else can you get an earful, a bellyful and a snootful at the same time?

—Gerald R. Ford

George Herter also mentioned that J.P.A. Martini's other alleged creation, the **Martini Verboten**, consisted of 2 oz. (60 ml) *genièvre* and 1 oz. (30 ml) apple cider vinegar.

and by accepting an appointment as the conductor of the Théâtre Feydeau.

Despite his strict religious upbringing, Martini was no different from his French art and music compatriots: He caroused and cavorted in the City of Light's numerous taverns. A far-fetched—even long-toothed—tale from the 1960s claims that Martini's favorite drink was a concoction made with *genièvre* and dry white wine. His friends dubbed this drink after its creator.

Unlike his many contemporaries who subscribed to the "live hard and die young" philosophy of most avant-garde creatives, the *genièvre*-drinking Martini lived to the ripe age of seventy-five. According to the tell tale, after his death in 1816, Martini's drink was often requested by Montmartre musicians and artists who exported the recipe to the New World as they sought their fame and fortune.

The teller of this long drink of a tale, George Leonard Herter, cited the *Nouveau Petit Larousse* as the source of his information. Ferreting through dusty bookshops and the National Bibliothèque in Paris as well as doling out euros to a private book seller, we procured a 1924 edition of this tome, only to find a small entry that mentioned Martini was the composer of two operas, *L'Amoureux de quinze* and *Plaisir d'amour*.

Still, it made for great small talk at the bar, we assure you. Back to reality. Now we will tell another tale about one of the Martini's supposed predecessors.

MARTINEZ

ATTRIBUTED TO JERRY "THE PROFESSOR" THOMAS

Many historians have attributed the Martini's origins to flamboyant bartender Jerry "the Professor" Thomas's creation—the Martinez. Curiously enough, in the 1862 edition of Thomas's *The Bar-Tender's Guide and Bon Vivant's Companion,* neither the Martini nor the Martinez is listed among the recipes. In fact, only ten cocktail recipes were presented: Bottle, Brandy, Fancy Brandy, Whiskey, Champagne, Gin, Fancy Gin, Japanese, Soda, and Jersey.

Gin Cocktails had been around for a while, making their way to New York where, in 1836, Irishman Tyrone Power commented that freed-slave and tavern owner Cato Alexander "was second to no man as a compounder of cock-tail, and such a hand at a gin-sling" at his tavern, Cato's Place, on the road between Manhattan and the Hudson Valley.

The Martinez was first documented in *The Modern Bartenders' Guide* by O. H. Byron, where it didn't give a recipe except to say that it was the "same as Manhattan, only you substitute gin for whiskey." The first recipe showed up in the posthumous 1887 revised and expanded edition of *The Bar-Tenders' Guide* that Thomas's publishers issued two years after his demise.

As far as we can reckon, much of the hype around the Martinez story was perpetrated by a 1965 *Oakland Tribune* article that disclosed the story of a young French bartender named Julio Richelieu, who had moved to Martinez, California, via New Orleans and married a local named Belinda Briones and opened a bar on Ferry Street. Then the following tale was told:

Shake

2 oz. (60 ml) Old Tom gin

0.5 oz. (15 ml) Martini & Rossi Rosso vermouth

2 dashes maraschino liqueur

3 drops Boker's Original Bitters

lemon slice

It is unlikely that the Martini evolved from the Martinez as the two drinks were first mentioned in print the same year, 1887, within months of each other.

Jerry Thomas's happy patrons toasted their camaraderie with a simple "Bottom's up."

WHAT'S OLD TOM GIN?

While most people seem to think it was a sweetened rotgut gin, that's only part of the story. Some Old Tom was simply cheap gin with sugar, just as some sparkling wines today are simply cheap wine that's been carbonated. Would you want to drink either of these? Of course not. On the other end of the scale, Old Tom was a nickname for cordial gin, which gained its sweetness from the botanicals used in its rectification. Then perhaps a little sugar was added on top of this already fine spirit.

Our favorite Lancashire-American bartender-author gaz regan (formerly known as Gary Regan) came up with a new old Martinez recipe after tasting some of the Old Tom reintroductions that have come on the market in the past few years. His **Ransom Martinez** stirs 2 oz. (60 ml) Ransom Old Tom Gin, 1 oz. (30 ml) Noilly Prat sweet vermouth, 0.25 oz. (10 ml) Luxardo maraschino liqueur, 2 dashes Angostura bitters, garnished with a lemon twist.

Richelieu dispensed Jessse Moore whiskey from a barrel only, serving customers by the shot glass. If a man wanted a bottle to take out he brought along his own empty bottle or else paid 25 cents for one of Julio's.

A miner, who said he was in a big hurry and didn't have an empty bottle with him, told Richelieu to take an extra small nugget for the container. At the door, with his purchase in hand, he turned and said:

"Bartender, don't you think I ought to get something extra for all that gold?"

Richelieu agreed and quickly mixed a few ingredients at random, including a green olive. . . .

The miner, who had watched his every move, tasted the mixture. Smacking his lips, he said, "What is this?"

"That," said Richelieu, "is a Martinez cocktail."

Now that we've found another clue to that drink's origin, let's look at who invented, or at least popularized, the Martini.

Jerry Thomas's **Gin Cocktail** mixed 2 drops Boker's Original Bitters, 4 oz. (120 ml) gin, 1–2 dashes Curaçao, and 3–4 dashes gomme syrup served in a standard glass.

Thomas's **Fancy Gin Cocktail** was made with the same ingredients but was served in a "fine wine glass." Both were shaken until ice cold and garnished with a lemon twist.

Audrey Saunders of Pegu Club divined a **Madeira Martinez** that stirs 2 oz. (60 ml) Blandy's 5-Year Bual Madeira, 1 oz. (30 ml) Beefeater gin, 0.5 tsp. honey syrup, 0.5 tsp. Al Wadi pomegranate molasses, 1 dash Angostura bitters, garnished with a bay leaf.

MARTINI COCKTAIL

DOCUMENTED BY HARRY "THE DEAN" JOHNSON

A man who was to be considered one of Thomas's contemporaries, Harry "the Dean" Johnson, did not have the Professor's P. T. Barnum entrepreneurial spirit. He is cherished for documenting in precise detail the setup and operation of a proper saloon. The 1882 edition of his drink book, *Harry Johnson's Bartenders' Manual, or How to Mix Drinks of the Present Style*, was funded by the International News Company, who printed fifty thousand copies. An obvious best seller, the 1888 edition added not only illustrations but contained detailed instructions for both the Martinez and the Martini among a few hundred other recipes. This was the first appearance in print of a Martini recipe, although the

Stir

1 oz. (30 ml) Old Tom gin

1 oz. (30 ml) Martini & Rossi Rosso vermouth

2 dashes gomme syrup

2 dashes Boker's Original Bitters

1 dash curaçao

Stir ingredients over ice and strain into a chilled cocktail glass.

A cocktail cherry or medium-size olive and squeeze a lemon twist over the top.

Back in the day, bartenders didn't wipe the entire rim of the glass with the lemon twist. They only wiped the side that would be away from the drinker. This puts the lemon in the nose where it belongs, not on the lips. The twist is all about the aroma, not the taste.

accompanying illustration was incorrectly captioned "Martine Cocktail."

However, it was not the only Martini recipe to appear in Johnson's opus. The Bradford à la Martini and Marguerite—the precursor to the Dry Martini—made their debut in this along with a few other drinks that followed the same gin-and-vermouth equation.

Was he the inventor? It's still a possibility. In the October 11, 1887, edition of the New York newspaper, *The Evening World*, an item about the offerings that William F. Mulhall, head bartender at the Hoffman House, served up noted: "Of course, the whiskey, Holland gin, Tom gin, hickory, Manhattan, Turf Club, vermouth, absinthe, Martini, and bourbon cocktails are served at all times, but several new ones which are growing in popularity are recent creations of Artist Mulhall."

We know that Johnson invented the Turf Club, the Bijou, and other gin-vermouth drinks. Why not the Martini? Then the question arose: Why Martini?

We aren't the only historians to ponder this question over a few Silver Bullets. The legend that the drink was named after the breech-loading Martini-Henry field rifle invented by Swiss designer Friedrich von Martini, which was adopted by the British military in 1871 and remained in service for thirty years, not only placed the drink's birth in Britain but on the surface was pretty far-fetched. (It's only by the grace of Lady Luck that no one paired the Martini automobile, built by Friedrich's son Adolph, which was placed in operation from 1897 to 1934, with the Silver Bullet.)

So why was the Martini christened the Martini?

We went back to Johnson's book and mused on the appearance of the Martini and the Bradford à la Martini. Why would anyone have an "à la Martini" recipe? We knew that there were other cocktails named after a featured product: The Bacardí Cocktail immediately came to mind. The Dubonnet Cocktail. So did the B&B (aka: Bénédictine and Brandy). The Havana Club Special.

Vermouth di Torino was a drink of choice, by the 1860s, in cafés throughout Europe. But patrons didn't ask for a glass of vermouth di Torino. They told the waiter: "A glass of Martini." Even today, if you ask for a Martini in just about any café in Lisbon, Barcelona, Paris, or Rome, chances are you'll get a glass of vermouth. You have to commend the Martini, Sola & Cia company for transforming its product into the first call brand.

In Johnson's day, New York City teemed with newly arrived emigrés hailing from vermouth-savvy countries including Harry's homeland—Germany. It's no surprise vermouth producers Cora, Carpano, and Dettone fared well at the 1853 Exhibition of the Industry of All Nations, staged within the majestic halls of the New York Crystal Palace.

Good publican that he was, Johnson devoted himself to making his guests happy. So why not craft a bunch of vermouth-laced cocktails? And why not a name that echoed a call that for many was reminiscent of home?

MARTINIS GO TO THE DOGS

At a banquet held at the Hotel Flanders, on November 22, 1899, for the Philadelphia Dog Show, the judges presented a first course of Blue Point oysters and Martini cocktails. These lucky banqueters also consumed potage à la Reine served with amontillado; terrapin served with Roderer Brut 1893 champagne; saddle of venison with Moët et Chandon Brut Imperial champagne; roast duck, fried hominy, and romaine salad; Brie and Stilton cheeses; and a bombe glacé accompanied by cordials. (And they wonder why we live longer these days.)

WHO CAME UP WITH THE OLIVE?

Just like the contenders to the throne of the Martini's originator, there are a few people cited as the inventor of the olive garnish, but one surfaces far more frequently than all the others combined.

John Doxat claimed that a friend of his interviewed a bartender who had once worked at the Hotel Knickerbocker with a barman by the name of Martini di Arma di Taggia, who told him that in 1910, he topped the Martini that he served to John D. Rockefeller with an olive. The millionaire had ordered a Gin-and-It. If it is not already clear these two stories are utter fiction, just look at some of the recipes from the 1890s. The Dry Martini had been born and the olive was already there before the Knickerbocker Hotel opened its doors.

Harry Johnson's **Bradford à la Martini** shook 1 oz. (30 ml) Old Tom gin, 1 oz. (30 ml) Italian vermouth, 4 dashes orange bitters, and the peel of one lemon in a mixing glass. Strained into a cocktail glass, it was garnished with an olive.

Johnson's **Bijou Cocktail** stirred 1 oz. (30 ml) Plymouth gin, 1 oz. (30 ml) Italian vermouth, 1 oz. (30 ml) green Chartreuse, and 1 dash orange bitters over ice. Strained into a cocktail glass, it was garnished with an olive and a lemon peel was squeezed over the top.

Parisian bar owner Louis Fouquet, in 1896, added a unique twist to his **Martini Cocktail**, mixing 4 dashes orange bitters, 2 dashes absinthe, 3 dashes curaçao, 3 dashes crème de noyaux, 1 oz. (30 ml) gin, and 1 oz. (30 ml) Italian vermouth. Strained into a cocktail glass, it was garnished with a lemon peel.

Created for American millionaire Harry Payne Whitney by Charlie at the New York Racquet Club, the **H.P.W.** shook 1.5 oz. (45 ml) Old Tom gin, and 1.5 oz. (45 ml) Italian vermouth.

The New York Racquet Club's signature **Racquet Club Cocktail** shook 2 oz. (60 ml) Plymouth gin, 1 oz. (30 ml) French vermouth, and 1 dash orange bitters.

The Crist Cocktail, a 1901 variation, stirred 3 dashes orange bitters, 1 dash maraschino liqueur, 1.5 oz. (45 ml) Tom gin, and 1.5 oz. (45 ml) French vermouth; stir well and strain into a cocktail glass.

Hidetsugu Ueno at Tokyo's Bar High Five makes his **Classic Gin Martini** by stirring 1.5 oz. (45 ml) Beefeater 47% over ice that's been rinsed with 0.5 oz. (15 ml) Dolin Extra-Dry vermouth and 4 atomizer sprays of Martini Bianco vermouth, garnished with an olive and a double lemon twist.

Peter Dorelli made the **Pebble Martini** in 1965 for the Pebble Bar at Stone's Chop House in London, stirring 2 oz. (60 ml) Booth's High & Dry gin, 0.5 oz. (15 ml) Noilly Prat dry vermouth, and 1 dash of Pernod.

MARGUERITE COCKTAIL

DOCUMENTED BY THOMAS STUART

The 1890s are often referred to as the "Gay Nineties." They should have been dubbed the "Dry Nineties" as far as cocktails were concerned. An early signal that the shift in public tastes moved from sweet to dry appeared in papers from coast to coast when premier American restaurateur John Chamberlin professed his preference in a poem that appeared in the October 11, 1891, edition of *New York World*.

I.—The Cocktail à la Chamberlin

Thrice happy man about to dine,
If you should luck that gift divine,
An appetite, to Plymouth gin
One drop of Curaçao to put in,
Of orange bitters then, forsooth,
Ten drops, and twice as much as
Vermouth,
A lemon peel should crown the
whole—
'Twill please the cockles of the soul.

This wasn't Chamberlin's only dictate on American cocktail tastes. He was probably the first to launch into a "That's not how you make a Martini!" rant, and the incident was reprinted in papers across the country off and on for a few years. In the winter of 1893–94, he ordered a drink in the café of the Hotel Bellevue in Philadelphia. While he was waiting for the waiter, a group of friends, journalists, joined him. He told them he had ordered a drink from his own restaurant's menu, the Waxem, and they decided to have the same. Before they could order, the waiter arrived with Chamberlin's drink. After a taste he shoved it back at the waiter saying,

Stir

2 oz. (60 ml) Plymouth gin

1 oz. (30 ml) Noilly Prat French vermouth

1 dash orange bitters

Further proof the olive was added as a matter of taste not "to cover up the raw taste of American gin" as has oft been repeated: At the time it found its way into the Martini, the top-selling gin in America wasn't bad, and wasn't even American. It was Plymouth.

"Take this thing back. I distinctly told you to request the barkeeper to use Plymouth gin and Italian vermouth in this cocktail. He has put in Holland gin and French vermouth and I wouldn't give ten cents for a hundred such concoctions."

The British Royal Navy's favorite gin, Plymouth Dry Gin, struck a strong chord on the taste buds of cocktail lovers and the minds of mixologists. Old Tom and Holland gin could not light a candle next to the floral aroma and delicate character of Plymouth Dry Gin. What Chamberlin didn't foresee was that his Plymouth and Italian call would morph even further within a few scant years.

The inroads made by Martini & Rossi's vermouth di Torino were quickly followed by Noilly Prat, French producer of a style that employed drier botanicals such as chamomile in its recipe. The two met up in the hands of the era's growing army of creative, masterful mixologists.

Thomas Stuart, in a 1904 reprint of his 1896 book *Stuart's Fancy Drinks and How to Mix Them,* provided a glimpse of the dryness to come with his streamlined recipe for the Marguerite Cocktail, which he listed under "New and Up-to-Date Drinks." You couldn't really call it a Martini, because it didn't contain that producer's product, at least for a few years.

Clean, clear, dry as dust, this 2:1 cocktail went by a different name as it was adopted in bar after bar—Miss Molly, Klondike Cocktail, Fairbanks Favorite—as it swept across the nation. Harry Johnson included his version as well as a variation called the Turf Cocktail in the 1900 revised edition of his blockbuster *Bartenders' Manual.*

So when did the Marguerite become the Dry Martini?

Harry Johnson's **Turf Cocktail** stirred 1 oz. (30 ml) Plymouth gin, 1 oz. (30 ml) French vermouth, 3 dashes orange bitters, 2 dashes maraschino, and 2 dashes absinthe, garnished with a medium-size olive.

Boston restaurateur Louis Muckensturm's **Marguerite Cocktail** stirred 2 oz. (60 ml) Plymouth gin, 1 oz. (30 ml) French vermouth, 1 dash maraschino, and 2 dashes orange bitters, served without a garnish.

The **Klondike Cocktail** that appeared in downtown New York bars in 1897 was "made preferably of gin, vermouth, and orange bitters . . . but the "Klondike suggestion" is given by floating a piece of lemon or orange peel cut into a disk and just the size of a $20 gold piece."

New York's Hoffman House served as its signature drink the **Hoffman House Cocktail**, which shook 2 oz. (60 ml) Plymouth gin, 1 oz. (3 ml) French vermouth, and 2 dashes orange bitters, garnished with a squeeze of lemon peel over the top.

DRY MARTINI COCKTAIL

DOCUMENTED BY LOUIS MUCKENSTURM

Stir

2 oz. (60 ml) dry gin

1 oz. (60 ml) French vermouth

2 dashes orange bitters

1 dash curaçao

Squeeze a piece of lemon peel
on top.

An 1895 joke (opposite
page) *may be pretty
tame, but it gets
immortalized here as the
first time the name Dry
Martini appeared in
print. It was also recycled
for the next few decades.
Change the name and
place and it was good to
go for a new generation
of Martini drinkers.*

He was white and shaken,
like a Dry Martini.

—P. G. Wodehouse,
Cocktail Time (1958)

Hats off to Boston restaurateur Louis Muckensturm for providing us with the first printed recipe in English for a 2:1 Dry Martini in his 1906 book *Louis' Mixed Drinks*. A respectful nod goes to Frank P. Newman, who published one in French for a 1:1 Dry Martini in his 1904 book *American-Bar, boissons anglaises et américaines*. (The first joke about a Dry Martini occurred in 1895.) But the real toast must be tipped to Martini & Rossi for its 1890 launch of Martini Extra-Dry Vermouth.

With a not-so-subtle marketing push, the clever early cocktail names were tossed aside at the turn of the century and the term "Martini" finally welded itself to this gin-vermouth libation when Martini & Rossi proclaimed in its 1906 nationwide ad campaign: "You cannot make a genuine 'Martini' (dry or otherwise) without Martini & Rossi Vermouth."

The company took a huge leap of faith when it produced the world's first commercial premixed cocktail in 1910—American Martini Cocktail. Signed on as its new American importer, the Heublein Company (you'll hear more about them later) got on the bottled cocktail bandwagon with its launch of Heublein Club Cocktails. Naturally, one of its first offerings was the Martini Cocktail.

Even the Martini's iconic stemmed cocktail glass got branded with a new identity. A passage from an item in the October 7, 1906, edition of New York's *The Sun* newspaper mentioned:

. . . the girl was fishing in the bottom of her Martini glass for the cherry at the very minute James was telling me how religious she was and how she sang in a choir and all that nonsense.

And here we thought the Martini glass was a modern slang expression.

A landmark bar opened in New York's Times Square just as Martini & Rossi's advertising campaign hit the streets in 1906. Built by John Jacob Astor IV, the Knickerbocker Hotel served as the background for a few Martini stories that we will now relate.

In its 1906 advertising campaign Martini & Rossi stirred its **Original Martini Cocktail** with 1 oz. (30 ml) Martini & Rossi vermouth, 2 oz. (60 ml) Tanqueray or other dry gin, squeeze of lemon peel, and a dash of orange bitters.

French hotelier Louis Leospo, in 1918, presented the **American Martini Cocktail**, which mixed 1 oz. (30 ml) Martini vermouth, 1 oz. (30 ml) gin, and 3 dashes orange bitters, served iced with a lemon peel.

Leospo's **Martini Cocktail #1** mixed 1 oz. (30 ml) Martini sweet vermouth, 1 oz. (30 ml) gin, and 3 dashes Angostura bitters, served iced with a lemon peel.

Leospo's **Martini Cocktail Dry** mixed 1 oz. (30 ml) Martini dry vermouth, 1 oz. (30 ml) gin, 3 dashes Angostura bitters, and 2 dashes curaçao, served iced with a lemon peel.

Peter Dorelli created a **3Ds Martini**, in 1967, while presiding at the Pebble Bar in Stone's Chop House, stirring 0.5 oz. (45 ml) Booth's High & Dry gin, 0.5 oz. (15 ml) Cinzano Bianco vermouth, 0.5 oz. (15 ml) Dubonnet, and 1 dash banana liqueur. (The 3Ds stood for Dorelli, [John] Doxat, and Dubonnet.)

His own **Leospo Cocktail** mixed 1 oz. (30 ml) Apéritif Rossi, 1 oz. (30 ml) gin, 2 dashes Angostura bitters, and 4 dashes curaçao, garnished with a grating of nutmeg and a lemon peel.

THE FIRST MARTINI JOKE

Thomas Q. Seabrooke yesterday hurriedly entered a small saloon on West Forty-second Street and ordered a Dry Martini cocktail.

"Vat you vant?" asked the proprietor.

"Dry Martini cocktail," said the actor, with laconic emphasis.

He then excused himself and said he would be back in a minute. When he returned he found three cocktails standing in a row. He looked about, but there was no one else in the saloon. He absorbed his stimulant and asked how much the charge was.

"Forty cents," replied the German.

"What! For one cocktail?" exclaimed Seabrooke.

"No, not *ein* cocktails, but *drei* cocktails. You said you wanted *drei* cocktails."

Seabrooke smiled sadly and paid the bill, leaving the other two cocktails to the astonished proprietor.

— *The New York World* (July 9, 1895)

By the time the first recipe titled "Dry Martini" was printed, the drink had been around for years. By 1902 you could buy it premixed in bottles. Dry Martinis were served as the opening toast at a 1902 banquet to welcome Prince Henny of Germany to New York (accompanied by caviar on toast, anchovies, and Blue Point oysters—yes, they knew what to serve with a Dry Martini!). In Maine, where they were still flirting with localized Prohibition, you could even find "chocolate drops filled with Dry Martinis."

One of my pet hates is that there are now so many so-called Martinis but for me any acceptable variation must include a vermouth to be called a Dry Martini.

—Peter Dorelli

Leospo's **Sweet Martini Cocktail** mixed 2 oz. (60 ml) Martini vermouth, 1 oz. (30 ml) gin, 2 dashes Angostura bitters, and 1 dash curaçao, served iced with a lemon peel.

Leospo's **Sweet Martini Cocktail for Ladies** mixed 2 oz. (60 ml) Martini vermouth vanilla, 1 oz. (30 ml) gin, 2 dashes Angostura bitters, and 3 dashes curaçao, served iced with a lemon peel.

The **Hawksmoor Martini** created by Richard Hunt at the Hawksmoor at Seven Dials in London shakes up 2 oz. (60 ml) Oxley gin, 0.5 oz. (15 ml) Cocchi Americano, 1 drop Difford's Christmas Bitters 2011, garnished with a clementine zest.

Pluck me ten berries from the juniper,
And in a beaker of strong barley spirit
The kindly juices of the fruit compress.
This is our Alpha. Next clap on your wings,
Fly South for Italy, nor come you back
'Til in the cup you have made prisoner
Two little thimblefuls of that sweet syrup
The Romans call Martini. Pause o'er Paris
And fill two eggshells with the French vermouth.
The home incontinent, and in one vessel
Cage your three captives, but in nice proportions,
So that no one is master, but the whole
Sweeter than France, but not so sweet as Italy.
Wring from an orange two bright tears, and shake,
Shake a long time the harmonious trinity,
Then in two cups like angels' tears present them,
And see there swims an olive in the bowl,
Which when the draught is finished shall remain
Like some sad emblem of perished love,
This is our Omega. Go, fellow!

—A. P. Herbert, "Let Us Have a Dry Martini,"
Providence News
(November 6, 1928)

FITTY-FITTY

CREATED BY AUDREY SAUNDERS AT PEGU CLUB, NEW YORK

She's only our utmost favorite living bartender in the entire world. And her place, Pegu Club, was our living room for the last two years that we lived in New York. (You could find us on the two bar stools nearest to the service bar at least twice a week. Never on a weekend, just during the week.)

We first met her when she was at the Tonic Restaurant, just before she took on the reopening of Bemelmans Bar at the Carlyle Hotel. (Lucky for us because it was a lot closer to our Upper West Side flat.) We've become close drinking buddies since those early days, sipping Manhattans topped with a splash of Bollinger in Midtown, Whiskey Sours in Moscow, Manhattans in the wilds of Herefordshire on the Welsh border, and scaring unwary bartenders with our exacting attitudes about how a Ramos Gin Fizz should be mixed. All in all, after all these years, we know why Audrey Saunders is known as the "Libation Goddess."

She knows not only how to peek deep into the soul of a classic, revisit its finer attributes, and come up with a classic of her own but also what every great bartender knows: how to serve that creation with warmth and love. Could you ask for much more?

When it comes to Martinis, she knows the drill: Everyone on the planet has an opinion of how the drink should be made. But even though we have our own fixed opinions on the subject, a Monday or a Wednesday night at Pegu was not complete unless one of us started with a

Stir

1.5 oz. (45 ml) Plymouth gin
1.5 oz. (45 ml) Dolin dry vermouth
1 dash Pegu orange bitters

lemon twist

How mayhem begins.

"No, I asked for the six-year whiskey, not six whiskies," Audrey said to the waitress with sigh of dismay, "Oh, put them down, I'll drink them."

Anistatia arrived late and the waitress caught her just as she reached the table and asked what Anistatia would like to drink. She gestured toward Audrey and said, "Oh, I'll have whatever she's having."

George Kappeler at New York's Holland House, in 1895, made his **Martini Cocktail** with 3 dashes orange bitters, 1 oz. (30 ml) Old Tom gin, 1 oz. (30 ml) Italian vermouth, and a piece of lemon peel, garnished with a maraschino cherry, if desired by the customer.

After Repeal, the **Fifty-Fifty** was streamlined to stir 1 oz. (30 ml) gin with 1 oz. vermouth, strained into a cocktail glass.

Fitty-Fitty served up in a Nick & Nora cocktail glass. (Taking a page from her program at Bemelmans, any leftovers that don't fit into the perfectly chilled glass are placed into a small decanter rested in a bowl of crushed ice.)

One of the many things we share in common is our appreciation of vermouth. And the Fitty-Fitty fulfills that appreciation of a forgotten ingredient in the cocktail lexicon. But we'll let her tell the story:

Before I opened Pegu in 2005, vermouth had become a defunct ingredient. I attributed this to the popularity of the Vodka Martini—the botanicals in gin have an affinity with the botanicals in vermouth, but do not pair at all well with vodka. Also you need to treat vermouth like wine, it needs to be fresh and this was not the case for many bars with dusty bottles of the stuff. At that time, my goal was to show everyone just how delicious vermouth could be, as well as showcase the beauty of this "forgotten" classic cocktail.

Originally I served this drink with Tanqueray and Noilly Prat. But at one point, Noilly changed its formula and the drink just didn't taste quite the same. So I switched to Dolin Dry for my house vermouth and reworked the cocktail, testing it with a number of different gins. Plymouth came out on top as pairing optimally with the Dolin.

See ya'll soon over a prime rib and a few Manhattans, Aud.

KNICKERBOCKER COCKTAIL

SIGNATURE DRINK AT THE HOTEL KNICKERBOCKER, NEW YORK

When John Jacob Astor IV opened his luxurious Knickerbocker Hotel, he was fortunate enough to to hire James B. Regan as his bar and restaurant manager. Regan had worked his way up from being a bar back at Earl's Hotel on Canal Street to a bartender post at the Hoffman House on Union Square before he became part-owner of the Pabst Rathskeller in Times Square. Taking up Astor's offer, Regan hired Eddie Woelke and a young Brit named Harry Craddock to man the bar, which served the likes of opera star Enrico Caruso (who lived in the hotel) and Astor himself, before his fateful death, in 1912, onboard the *Titanic*.

The Knickerbocker's signature offering was a Martini variation that derived its rosy hue from a dash of Italian vermouth added to an otherwise Dry Martini.

When Regan retired, in 1920, the hotel closed. Eddie Woelke had left a couple years earlier, stepping into the limelight as bartender in Havana's Sevilla-Biltmore Hotel and creator of the rum version of the Martini—El Presidente. After cutting his bartending teeth in the United States for twenty-two years, British ex-pat Harry Craddock took his wife and stepdaughter home to the United Kingdom, where he got a job at the American Bar in London's Savoy Hotel.

We'll tell you more about Harry after we narrate a tall tale that also grew around the Knickerbocker's bar and the Martini.

Author John Doxat dramatized a handed down story in his 1972 book *Drinks and Drinking* about the Martini's

Shake
2 oz. (60 ml) dry gin
1 oz. (30 ml) French vermouth
1 dash Italian vermouth

Squeeze a lemon peel over the top.

American journalist Carl Helm used to tell a story about Enrico Caruso's cocktail preference at the Knickerbocker. According to Helm, as related by columnist Bob Considine who was introduced to Martinis by Helm, ". . . the great tenor gave instructions to the bar at the old Knickerbocker Hotel to keep his martini glasses stuffed bowl-down for several hours in shaved ice over which the bartender would occasionally spray a bit of absinthe. It permeated the frosty glass."

birth that clung to the drink's legend until the mid-1990s. As Doxat tells it, his friend James Porter recorded an interview in the early 1970s with an aged bartender named Luigi who was in his last years before retirement behind the bar at Genoa's Savoia Majestic Hotel.

Luigi apparently immigrated to the United States in 1912, where he managed to secure a bar back post at the Knickerbocker Hotel, working with "Signor Martini" (aka: Martini di Arma di Taggia), who taught him how to make a Martini. The aspiring young bartender had been told by di Taggia that, in 1910, millionaire John D. Rockefeller walked into the bar. His usual call was for a Gin-and-French, but di Taggia made him a Martini with an olive instead.

Never mind that the Martini and the Dry Martini had been around and in print for a few years before Luigi arrived in New York. Never mind that the tale was handed down from a very old and very romantic bartender to a businessman sitting in his bar who told it to his wartime buddy John Doxat, who committed the story to print. Every once in a while, you'll walk into a bar and still hear a reiteration of Luigi's tale.

The American Bar at the Savoy's Harry Craddock presented a **Perfect Cocktail**, which shook 1 oz. (30 ml) dry gin, 1 oz. (30 ml) French vermouth, and 1 oz. (30 ml) Italian vermouth.

The legendary Dale DeGroff prefers a **Knickerbocker Dry Oliver Twist**, stirring 1 oz. (30 ml) dry gin, 1 oz. (30 ml) French vermouth, and 2 dashes of his personal orange bitters, garnished with an olive and a lemon twist. (See page 197 for his personal bitters recipe.)

GIBSON COCKTAIL

CREATED FOR WALTER D. K. GIBSON AT THE BOHEMIAN CLUB, SAN FRANCISCO

Ever wonder who invented the Gibson? It's the drink Roger Thornhill ordered in the dining car of the 20th Century Limited train in the 1959 Alfred Hitchcock film *North by Northwest*. Bette Davis downs one in *All About Eve* before she says, "Fasten your seat belts, it's going to be a bumpy night." (Right after that, a very young Marilyn Monroe makes a brief appearance.)

There are a bunch of stories about the Gibson. The one most commonly bandied about is that the Gibson is named after Charles Dana Gibson, American illustrator and creator of the Gibson Girls.

Journalist Lucius Beebe started one rumor in his 1946 *The Stork Club Bar Book* that the illustrator "evolved" the drink at the bar in New York's Plaza Hotel—the same place Thornhill ordered one in the movie. (But the Plaza didn't open until 1907.)

Another Gibson story was that he liked to drink with friends at the Players Club on Gramercy Park South in New York. To remain clear-headed enough to return to his latest illustration, he worked out a code with the club's bartender, Charley Connolly: His Martini was nothing but ice water, and Charlie "marked it" by using a cocktail onion instead of an olive as garnish. His friends quickly caught on—not to the code, but to the garnish. Lauding his inventiveness, they ordered their Martinis with cocktail onions: "Charley, gimme a Gibson."

Shake

2 oz. (60 ml) Plymouth dry gin

1 oz. (30 ml) Martini & Rossi extra-dry vermouth

cocktail onion

Famed food writer M.F.K. Fisher–a regular Dry Martini drinker–wrote that the best Martini she'd ever had was served to her at the Antlers Hotel in Colorado Springs. The bar's secrets to making an **Antlers Dirty Gibson**: an onion garnish and a teaspoon of the onion brine added to the gin and French vermouth. Fisher later insisted the cocktail onions must be imported from the Netherlands.

Charles McCabe interviewed Charles Gibson's father, Allan P. Gibson, and included this same story in his December 9, 1968, column as well as in his 1974 book The Good Man's Weakness.

Wine and vermouth are not the only alcoholic beverages that change with age. Distilled spirits also tend to improve over time, especially in unopened bottles. As long as the liquid level has not dropped more than a centimeter (two at the most), the flavor will usually be sweeter and more refined in an old bottle of spirits. However, if the bottle was stored on its side with liquid in contact with a cork for decades or if the seal wasn't up to the job and the liquid evaporated down to two-thirds or half its original level, the flavor is likely to be pretty bad (this is why old cognacs are stored upright, and consumed quickly if the level starts to drop).

Another fairy tale says that the double cocktail onion garnish paid homage to the physical assets of Gibson's beautiful models—the belles of the 1890s.

One question: What's an illustrator doing at the Players Club? Why wasn't he sipping next door at the National Arts Club, where he could rub elbows with fellow artists and their patrons?

Cocktail writer Colleen Graham was contacted in 2006 by Charles Pollock Gibson, who repeated an oral history about his father's great-uncle, businessman Walter D. K. Gibson. It seems that the elder Gibson frequented San Francisco's Bohemian Club, around 1898, but did not like the bartender's method for making a Martini. Gibson preferred his Silver Bullet to be made with Plymouth gin and stirred. *The Wall Street Journal*'s Eric Felten also concurred in 2009, citing an 1898 item written by a Bohemian Club member as the first printed reference to the event.

For a pop-up restaurant held at London's Sipsmith Distillery in 2009, Jared created a **Shinkansen Martini**, shaking 1 oz. (30 ml) Sipsmith dry gin and 1 oz. (30 ml) shiso-infused shochu, garnished with sweet pickled scallions. (See page 196 for the shiso-infused shochu recipe.)

The Old Army Cocktail shook 2 oz. (60 ml) gin, 1 oz. (30 ml) Italian vermouth, 2 lemon twists, and an orange twist, garnished with a cocktail onion.

The gin was gone, but the vermouth was still available in the United States during Prohibition. Martini & Rossi and other companies produced nonalcoholic vermouth for the American market. Even so, it was not frequently found in speakeasies as proprietors knew not just the alcohol would be confiscated. Law enforcement officers took anything that was in a bottle and either impounded it as evidence or smashed it on the spot. Why keep a load of expensive products in the bar that people aren't specifically coming to drink? Olives, according to one speakeasy denizen, were another rare product.

I personally like the **Martini Sandwich** that H. L. Mencken talked about that is a 3:1 Dry Martini with a small glass of beer served on either side of it.

—Angus Winchester

You can't really beat straight premium vodka. I'm a big fan of Ketel One with lots of cocktail onions. It's like a Martini Salad.

—Loren Dunsworth, Lola's Restaurant, West Hollywood

Some say that another member of the Players Club, actor Cyril Cusack, introduced the Gibson to Murphy's Bar in Dublin, where the owner—who was out of cocktail onions—stuck a fresh radish in the drink instead. With that, the **Murphy Cocktail** was born.

Our own version—the **Dirty Gibson**—combines 1 oz. (30 ml) Beefeater London Dry Gin, 0.5 oz. (15 ml) Martini & Rossi extra-dry vermouth, and a splash of cocktail onion brine with a cocktail onion garnish.

Sasha Petraske of Milk & Honey makes a **Spring Forward**, which is a Gibson variation that stirs 1 oz. (30 ml) gin and 0.5 oz. (15 ml) bianco vermouth. Press a 2-inch piece of scallion or spring onion into the mixing glass before stirring and icing. Garnish with another piece of scallion or spring onion.

This Gibson story makes more sense, but this puzzle's not solved yet. The first time a Gibson cocktail was mentioned in print was 1898, in New York. Edward W. Townsend, columnist for *The World,* created a fictional society couple named Major Max and his wife. He transcribed their breakfast banter for *World* readers. When the wife inquired about Colonial Holland, Major Max replied, "Colonial Holland is a very superior article of gin, my dear, which, if mixed properly with an equal part of dry vermouth and properly chilled makes a Gibson cocktail." But New York? Hats off to Felten for discovering Townsend was a former vice president of the Bohemian Club recently transplanted to New York.

YALE COCKTAIL

Then came Prohibition. Americans were forced underground (and abroad) in search of their Fizzes, Rickeys, Slings, and Martinis after the Eighteenth Amendment (aka: the Volstead Act) went into effect on January 16, 1920. The resulting ban on the manufacture and sale of alcoholic beverages did more than make outlaws out of upstanding American citizens, it birthed a new counterculture of mobsters, rumrunners, flappers, and playboys.

Many Americans devised ways to "sneak a belt of the sauce." Bootleggers crisscrossed the Canadian and Mexican borders and rumrunners braved the waters of the Caribbean and the Gulf of Mexico, while bathtub gin makers conjured up moonshine-quality hooch. Designer hip flasks became standard fashion accessories. Daily seaplane flights whisked thirsty Americans to Cuba from as far away as Detroit. Smoky speakeasies—where the underworld rubbed shoulders with freewheeling socialites—and some savvy restaurants had ingenious ways of outsmarting law enforcers, serving cocktails in coffee cups and concealing their bars behind hidden panels.

Thinly veiled schemes like the "blind pig" and "blind tiger" emerged. A beer garden or outdoor bar would be set up. Patrons would pay fifteen cents to get a look at a blind pig or some other non-attraction displayed in one corner of the space. Of course, a free drink was included with every admission.

Shake

2 oz. (60 ml) dry gin

3 dashes Angostura bitters

1 dash orange bitters

Squeeze a lemon peel over the top.

Forty miles from whisky,
And sixty miles from gin
I'm leaving this damn
country
For to live a life of sin.

—Anonymous

According to Groucho Marx, W. C. Fields kept about $50,000 worth of booze stashed in his attic: "Don't you know that Prohibition is over?" Groucho asked. "Well, it may come back!" Fields replied.

Why don't you get out of that wet coat and into a Dry Martini?

—*The Major and the Minor*
(1942)

CHARLES
BUTTERWORTH:
You ought to get out of those wet clothes and into a Dry Martini.

—*Every Day's a Holiday*
(1937)

*Robert Benchley's
Martini formula was
"gin, and just enough
vermouth to take away
that nasty, watery look."*

This sign appeared in Boston barroom windows in the months leading up to Prohibition: "We stole this country from the Indians. They can have it back in July."

More than a few Ivy Leaguers at Princeton and Yale applied their chemistry education to quench their desires, distilling their own bootleg liquor. But there was a hitch. Without the controlled conditions and secret formulae used by legitimate distillers, most bathtub gin tasted more like liniment than liquor. (That's what happens when you mix industrial-grade alcohol with glycerine and juniper oil.)

Prohibition bolstered attendance at private clubs and country clubs, where stockpiles of booze that had been imported before the Volstead Act was enforced were shaken and stirred by top bartending talents. Another bastion, the White House, wasn't without its stock of alcohol either. Word leaked out that President Warren G. Harding drank and smoked his way through his single term in office. So did Franklin Delano Roosevelt's predecessor Herbert Hoover, who was purportedly a Martini lover. (Calvin Coolidge learned from Harding's media mishap and allegedly remained sober throughout his term.)

Artists and intellectuals seemed to have solid connections to the underground liquor supply. It was during this time that *The New Yorker* magazine's book reviewer Dorothy Parker scribed her Martini dedication:

> I love to drink Martinis,
> Two at the very most
> Three, I'm under the table
> Four, I'm under the host.

Incidentally, that was far from Ms. Parker's raciest outburst. We like this one: "If all the girls who attended the Yale prom were laid end-to-end, I wouldn't be surprised."

It started as a one-hour roast of New York theater critic Alexander Woollcott, but the infamous Round Table's ten-year-long lunch at New York's Algonquin Hotel became the stuff of legend. Critics like Parker and Woollcott were joined by columnist Franklin Pierce Adams, playwrights Marc Connelly, Robert E. Sherwood, and George S. Kaufman, writer/actor Robert Benchley, *The New Yorker* editor Harold Ross, writer Ruth Hale, and publicist John Peter Toohey (who started the whole mess). Besides hurling memorable innuendoes and venomous insinuations in the hotel's Rose Room, the Round Table frequently adjourned upstairs to drink Martinis and play poker.

Cocktails continued to play an important role in the group's gatherings at their private retreat—Neshobe Island in Vermont. "Dinner on the island was only part of the evening ritual," Round Table member Harpo Marx recalled. "The first ceremony at day's end, for which everybody gathered in the clubhouse, was cocktails."

An occasional Round Table guest, British novelist P. G. Wodehouse, also contributed a few Martinis to the era's literature, creating characters like the amiable member of Britain's idle rich, Bertie Wooster, who regularly lubricated himself with Dry Martinis and many similar drinks masterfully mixed by his valet (and often savior) Jeeves.

Wodehouse and another Round Table guest, playwright/actor Noël Coward, were no strangers to cocktails. On the contrary, they had plenty of places to whet their whistles back home in the Big Smoke's West End.

A Prohibition toast: "Here's to Carrie Nation, of anti-drink renown, though against libation, she hit every joint in town."

Author Finis Farr was an occasional diner at the Algonquin Round Table. We can thank him for calling the Martini "the breakfast of champions."

"I'd gotten all set up for a day of fishing," the old angler said to his friends. "Found a perfect riverbank under a willow tree, had a cooler with all the fixings and made myself a perfect Martini, when I realized I'd forgotten to bring bait. Just then I spotted a small snake with a big minnow in its mouth slithering out of the water. I caught it and took the minnow to use for bait. But I felt so guilty about stealing the snake's breakfast that I poured a few drops of my Martini into his mouth before I let him go. Half an hour later I felt something against my leg. I glanced down, and here's that same snake, back with three more minnows."

—Jared Brown

Yale University had one and so did its New Jersey archrival. The **Princeton Cocktail** shook 1.5 oz. (45 ml) dry gin, 1 oz. (30 ml) dry vermouth, and 1 oz. (30 ml) fresh lime juice.

A post-Prohibition version of the **Princeton Cocktail** stirred 2 oz. (60 ml) Old Tom gin, 1 oz. (30 ml) port wine, and 2 dashes orange bitters, garnished with a lemon twist.

A 1933 cocktail competition, held under the National Association for the Advancement of the Fine Art of Drinking banner, took place in Carmel, California. Authors Sinclair Lewis and Edgar Rice Burroughs competed against humorist J. P. McEvoy, among others. The winner was Washington political writer Samuel G. Blythe. Blythe, who'd purportedly been on the wagon since 1911, dubbed his creation the merry-go-round cocktail: "one-sixth Italian vermouth, one-sixth French vermouth (both to be genuine), two-thirds London dry gin (also genuine). Mix with spoon in tall glass filled with ice. One good sized olive in each cocktail. Squeeze of lemon peel over top of each cocktail." Sounds perfect!

HANKY-PANKY COCKTAIL

CREATED BY ADA COLEMAN, THE AMERICAN BAR AT THE SAVOY HOTEL, LONDON

Hotelier Rupert D'Oyly Carte was a chip off the old block. His theatrical impresario dad, Richard, made a fortune producing Sir William S. Gilbert and Arthur Sullivan's light operas—*The Mikado, Pirates of Penzance,* et al.—at his Savoy Theatre on London's Strand. A Victorian visionary, Richard built a hotel next to his theatre, in 1889, that sported electric lights, elevators, and an en-suite bath in every room—the first British hotel to offer such luxuries. He followed up that financial success, in 1893, with the purchase and retrofitting of its rival hotel, Claridge's. He closed the place for five years so he could install the same amenities into new property. He also closed the Savoy around the same time to add a few more elaborate touches.

When both hotels reopened, in 1898, each sported yet another luxurious amenity—an American Bar. Claridge's also sported another first: Richard hired a female bartender named Ada Coleman.

Richard died three years later and his son Rupert took over the family's hotel empire and theater enterprise. He also mentored Ada in her career, in 1903, installing her at the Savoy's American Bar. Coley, as she was known by her regulars, served a cavalcade of A-listers, including Mark Twain, the Prince of Wales, and stage actor/theater manager Sir Charles Hawtrey, who mentored Noël Coward's career.

We have to thank Hawtrey for walking into the American Bar and saying: "Coley, I am tired. Give me something with a bit of punch in it." She spent hours

Shake

1 oz. (30 ml) dry gin

1 oz. (30 ml) Italian vermouth

2 dashes Fernet Branca

Squeeze an orange peel over the top.

Over at London's Royal Automobile Club bartender Robert Vermeire mixed up a **Gloom Raiser**, in 1915, stirring 1 oz. (30 ml) dry gin, 1 oz. (30 ml) Noilly Prat dry vermouth, 2 dashes grenadine, and 2 dashes absinthe.

In the United States, Jack Townsend's 1950s version of the **Fourth Estate** shook 1 oz. (30 ml) dry gin, 1 oz. (30 ml) French vermouth, 1 oz. (30 ml) Italian vermouth, and 3 dashes absinthe.

playing around with recipes and the next time he walked in, she presented him with her creation. He sipped it. Then, draining the glass he exclaimed, "By Jove! That is the real hanky-panky!" The name stuck.

Ada Coleman handed over her head bartender mantel, in 1923, to a repatriating Brit who sought solace from America's Prohibition. Under his guidance, the cocktail's golden age survived in Britain, fueling a generation of Bright Young People to party until dawn in the West End's finest watering holes.

Harry Craddock's predecessor behind the bar at the Savoy, Ada Coleman was more than the world's first female bartender. A 1926 poll found her to be considered the world's best bartender. However, she was not behind the bar on her own. For more than twenty years, she worked side by side with another female bartender, Ruth Burgess. Prior to Prohibition, Americans were horrified that this British tradition of barmaids might spread to the United States, where bartending was a strictly male profession.

Named after Senator Charles Warren Fairbanks, the **Fairbanks Cocktail** stirred 1 oz. (30 ml) dry gin, 1 oz. (30 ml) French vermouth, 2 dashes Noyau Rosé, and 2 dashes orange bitters, garnished with a squeeze of orange peel over the top.

Vermeire's **Yellow Rattler** stirred 1 oz. (30 ml) dry gin, 1 oz. (30 ml) Italian vermouth, 1 dash orange bitters, and a small "bruised" white onion.

The American Bar at the Savoy's Harry Craddock came up with the **Rolls-Royce Cocktail**, which shook 1 oz. (30 ml) dry gin, 0.5 oz. (15 ml) French vermouth, 0.5 oz. (15 ml) Italian vermouth, and 1 dash Bénédictine.

CORPSE REVIVER #2

Born in Burleigh, Gloucestershire, in 1897, Harry Craddock sought his fortune on the other side of "the Pond" when he turned twenty-one years old. Landing in New York, he made his way west, working in bars at Cleveland's Hollenden Hotel and Chicago's Palmer House Hotel before taking a post at New York's Hoffman House, Holland House, and the Hotel Knickerbocker. Prohibition went into effect in January 1920 and by April, Harry high-tailed it home to Britain—the land of whiskey and soda drinkers, who, in his mind, couldn't care less about cocktails.

Harry was on a mission to save the cocktail's honor. Replacing Coley at the Savoy's American Bar, Craddock exploited the lessons he'd learned about public relations while living in America. The British

Shake

0.5 oz. (15 ml) dry gin

0.5 oz. (15 ml) Kina Lillet

0.5 oz. (15 ml) Cointreau

0.5 oz. (15 ml) fresh lemon juice

1 dash absinthe

I never go jogging, it makes me spill my Martini.

—George Burns

The way to drink a cocktail is quickly, while it's still laughing at you.

—Harry Craddock

The **Twentieth Century Cocktail** shook 1.5 oz. (45 ml) Plymouth gin, 0.5 oz. (15 ml) crème de cacao, 0.75 oz. (20 ml) Kina Lillet, and 0.5 oz. (15 ml) fresh lemon juice, garnished with a lemon twist.

The **Chorus Lady** shook 1 oz. (30 ml) dry gin, 1 oz. (30 ml) French vermouth, and 1 oz. (30 ml) Italian vermouth with the juice of an orange quarter, garnished with an orange slice and a cocktail cherry.

The **Boulevard Cocktail** shook 1 oz. (30 ml) dry gin, 0.5 oz. (15 ml) fresh orange juice, 0.5 oz. (15 ml) dry vermouth, and 0.5 oz. (15 ml) Italian vermouth.

Mauro Mahjoub, who owns Mauro's Negroni Club in Munich, Germany, favors a **Dusty Martini**, stirring 2 oz. (60 ml) Plymouth gin, 0.5 oz. (15 ml) Lillet Blanc, 1 dash orange bitters, and 1 dash apple juice. The mixing glass is rinsed with Galliano before the rest of the ingredients go inside. The finished drink is garnished with an orange twist and a pinch of ground cinnamon.

took note. Dubbed the "cocktail king" by the International News Service, Craddock boasted of mixing at least one hundred thousand cocktails for the Savoy's American guests and a few thousand more for "visitors of other nationalities." Word got out that he went into training two weeks before the "cocktail season," working out at the gym for three hours in the morning and three hours in the afternoon just so he could be in peak condition.

London bartenders upped their game as the 1920s unfolded, serving the Bright Young People (aka: Bright Young Things) an incredible repertoire of cocktails. The tabloids couldn't get enough of their antics or the places they haunted. Neither could novelists P. G. Wodehouse, Evelyn Waugh, and Nancy Mitford. Neither could photographer Cecil Beaton. On any given night the Café Royal, the Berkeley, Ciro's Club, Claridge's, the Dorchester, the Ritz, Quaglino's, and, oh yes, the Savoy were packed with the prettiest, the wittiest, and the brightest, who all clamored for cocktails.

Paying homage to Noël Coward's 1925 West End theatrical hit, Craddock's **Fallen Angel** shook 2 oz. (60 ml) dry gin, 1 oz. (30 ml) fresh lemon juice, 1 dash Angostura bitters, and 2 dashes crème de menthe.

Named after the New York borough zoo, Nassau Gun Club's **Bronx Cocktail** shook 1 oz. (30 ml) dry gin, 0.5 oz. (15 ml) French vermouth, 0.5 oz. (15 ml) Italian vermouth, and the juice of an orange quarter. This same drink also went by the name the **Bronx Express**.

Paying homage to American cowboy comedian and sage, the **Will Rogers Cocktail** shook 1 oz. (30 ml) Plymouth gin, 0.5 oz. (15 ml) French vermouth, 0.5 oz. (15 ml) fresh orange juice, and 4 dashes curaçao.

ARNAUD MARTINI

SELECTED BY BOOTH'S GIN FOR ACTRESS YVONNE ARNAUD, LONDON

For those who couldn't afford to trip the light fantastic at Ciro's, the Café Royal, or the Savoy—or simply wanted to continue the festivities at home—dozens of cocktail books and booklets were printed to help aspirants mix their own. *An Anthology of Cocktails, Together with Selected Observations by a Distinguished Gathering, and Diverse Thoughts for Great Occasions*—a booklet produced by Booth's gin—was one notable contribution. This slim volume presented British theatrical, sports, and social celebrities, their endorsed recipes and comments, and a handy map that pinpointed the location of twenty-two trendy West End drinking establishments.

Ivor Novello, West End theater idol and star of an early Alfred Hitchcock film, was given the Star Cocktail. One of

Shake
1 oz. (30 ml) Booth's gin
1 oz. (30 ml) French vermouth
1 oz. (30 ml) crème de cassis

Laugh and the world laughs with you—drink and it does the same.

—Tom Walls,
An Anthology of Cocktails
(c. 1920s)

H. L. Mencken, while researching the etymology of the word "cocktail" for his monumental work **The American Language**, hired a mathematician to calculate how many different cocktails could be mixed from the stock of a first-class bar. The answer was 17,864,392,788.

—John Watney,
Mother's Ruin (1976)

Not that you need an excuse to to raise a Martini toast, but here are a few exceptional days for doing so:

National Martini Day (U.S.), June 19
Dorothy Parker's birthday, August 22
Harry Johnson's birthday, August 28
Harry Craddock's birthday, August 29
Repeal Day, December 5

For Dame Sybil Thorndike's guests, the company selected a then-modern take on the **Trilby Cocktail**, which shook 1 oz. (30 ml) Booth's gin, 1 oz. (30 ml) Italian vermouth, and 2 dashes orange bitters.

The original **Trilby Cocktail** created by Harry Johnson stirred 1 oz. (30 ml) blended Scotch whiskey, 1 oz. (30 ml) Italian vermouth, 2 dashes absinthe, 2 dashes orange bitters, and 2 dashes Parfait d'Amour, garnished with cherries and a squeeze of lemon peel over the top.

playwright George Bernard Shaw's favorite muses actress Dame Sybil Thorndike was honored with the Trilby.

Our personal favorite, though, was the drink conferred on West End actress Yvonne Arnaud. (We have to take a moment here to apologize to readers of the first edition of *Shaken Not Stirred*® : *A Celebration of the Martini.* We speed-researched—without the aid of our now voluminous personal library—and speed-wrote that manuscript in the midst of excessive research and testing, and we accidentally called this drink the Arnaud Cocktail. In the Booth's *Anthology* booklet, the drink was actually called the Parisian. Sorry about that. But hey, it's nice to see it appear as the Arnaud on cocktail menus in as far-flung places as Boise, London, Melbourne, Amsterdam, and New York. You won't find one at Arnaud's Restaurant in New Orleans, however. There, they make an Arnaud's Special Cocktail that features blended Scotch and Dubonnet.)

In the same book, the company selected a drink for composer/ film actor Ivor Novello called **The Star Cocktail**, which shook 1 oz. (30 ml) Booth's gin, 1 oz. (30 ml) calvados, 1 dash French vermouth, 1 dash Italian vermouth, and 1 tsp. fresh grapefruit juice.

The Nassau Gun Club in Princeton, New Jersey, made a completely different **Star Cocktail** that featured applejack and Italian vermouth with equal billing.

DIRTY MARTINI

Ever wonder what it was that made Franklin Delano Roosevelt such a popular U.S. president? Okay, so there was the New Deal, the end of the Great Depression, his pro-workingman approach to domestic policy, his warm and accessible public persona, and his remarkable personal strength as demonstrated in his determination to overcome physical challenges. But Roosevelt also signed the order to repeal Prohibition, shook the first legal post-Prohibition Martini, and had a talent few commanders-in-chief possessed. Perhaps Noël Coward put it best:

> [Roosevelt's] study was typical of him, I think. It was furnished unpretentiously and in quiet taste . . . His desk was solid and business-like, although at the moment it had banished affairs of state for the day and given itself up to frivolity, for it was littered with an elaborate paraphernalia of cocktail implements. There were bottles, glasses of different sizes for short and long drinks, dishes of olives and nuts and cheese straws, also an ice bucket, a plate of lemons with a squeezer, a bowl of brown sugar, two kinds of bitters and an imposing silver shaker. Among all these the President's hands moved swiftly and surely; they . . . never erred, whether he happened to be looking at what he was doing or not. He was evidently proud of his prowess as a barman, as indeed he had every reason to be . . .

Roosevelt brandished his cocktail shaker for heads of state and distinguished guests throughout his terms in office. He personally favored Old-Fashioneds and

Shake
1.5 oz. (45 ml) dry gin
0.5 oz. (15 ml) French vermouth
1 tsp. olive brine

stuffed green olive

Rub the glass rim with a lemon twist before pouring and garnishing.

Appropriate toasts to FDR's favorite Martini include:
Happy days are here again!
To the New Deal!
To the Working Man!

We do have one word of caution if you plan to stack your olives on a toothpick: Make sure you don't consume the implement along with your veggies. (Author Sherwood Anderson made that literally fatal mistake while partaking of his daily Martini meal.)

Dirty Martinis, but according to some sources, he occasionally strayed by adding a splash of orange juice, grapefruit juice, or anisette to his Martini.

We don't know who started the rumor that the first drink President Franklin Delano Roosevelt shook as the clock struck midnight, heralding the end of Prohibition, was a Dirty Martini. But it makes a great bar story.

Jared has another take on the subject:

I didn't know what a Dirty Martini was, but two very attractive women a few seats down from me at the bar ordered a few rounds. Each time they gave the bartender a lascivious wink and a smile. Certain I had stumbled on some sado-sexual secret society's signal I watched out of the corner of my eye as he mixed a round for them. Sure enough, he ladled a spoonful of some unrecognizable clear liquid from below the bar into their glasses. I guess they spotted me, because they told the bartender to make one for me, too. Caught! I was tempted to make a run for it, but curiosity got the best of me. Don't know if I was more relieved or disappointed to discover that it was just a standard see-through with extra olive brine. However, it makes for a darned good Martini! Later, I discovered you could order them R, X, or XXX rated depending on how dirty you like them.

THE ASTORIA COCKTAIL

Shake

1 oz. (30 ml) Old Tom gin

2 oz. (60 ml) French vermouth

2 dashes Abbott's orange bitters

I'm not talking a cup of cheap gin splashed over an ice cube. I'm talking satin, fire, and ice; Fred Astaire in a glass; surgical cleanliness; insight and comfort; redemption and absolution. I'm talking a Martini.

—Anonymous

Thanks to President Roosevelt, cocktails were back on the menu across America. Hotels snapped up the seasoned bartenders from Europe, speakeasies disappeared or were transformed into legit establishments, railway companies hired professional barmen for their elegant club cars. The Orient Express wasn't the world's only deluxe passenger train. Noël Coward frequently toured the United States, taking the Twentieth Century Limited from New York to Chicago and the Super Chief from Chicago to Los Angeles. Like his fellow passengers—millionaires, actors, and writers—Coward reveled in the quality of the American rail service, commenting:

> The over-luxurious journey from New York to Chicago in the 'Twentieth Century'; the red carpet laid across the platform; the obsequious coloured porters in their white coats; the deep armchair in the club car; the superlatively dry dry Martini before dinner; the dinner itself, perfectly served and of such infinite variety so far removed from the sullen table d'hôtes of our own dear Southern [British] Railway ...

The public at large couldn't afford to drink a lot, it was the Great Depression, ya know. Those who wanted to try their hand at shaking and stirring at home had plenty of help from cocktail books pouring in from Europe and locally written by veteran bartenders and published by the dozens, and cocktail shakers that had recipes printed or engraved on them. Bartenders like Oscar at New York's Waldorf-Astoria Hotel were more than happy to share

Hal Boyle—who in his thirty years as an Associated Press columnist, produced 7,680 columns appearing in more than 700 newspapers, comprising a total output of four times as many words as Shakespeare—had a lot to say about Martinis (certainly more than the great bard had to say about them). In one column he interviewed Eustace Scannell, formerly of the IRS's Alcohol Tax Unit, who had conducted an extensive study of the Martini. He found the optimal serving temperature was 38°F (3.3°C). His perfect gin to vermouth ratio, in 1955, matched our 2011 survey on Facebook. He said at 3:1 it tastes like vermouth, and at 4:1 it tastes like gin. At 3.5:1 the drink is balanced between them. He also said, "Anybody who puts either an olive or a piece of lemon peel in his Martini is only compromising with perfection."

their wisdom with the latest generation of cocktail-swigging Americans. Oscar also shared one hundred recipes for the drinks he claimed were made famous at the Waldorf-Astoria, including the Astoria.

The cocktail party may have been invented before Prohibition, and had been the way to go during Prohibition if you didn't want to get caught in a raid on your local speakeasy. With Repeal, the cocktail party gathered new purpose and meaning. A gentleman's or a lady's ability to mix a Martini for guests at home was a symbol of civility, of a person who knew how to appreciate the finer things in life.

Before the decade was out, a not so subtle change happened to the Martini.

New York's Plaza Hotel had its **Plaza Cocktail**, which shook 1 oz. (30 ml) dry gin, 1 oz. (30 ml) French vermouth, 1 oz. (30 ml) Italian vermouth with a pineapple slice.

London's Savoy had its **Savoy Hotel Special Cocktail (No. 1)**, which shook 2 oz. (60 ml) dry gin, 1 oz. (30 ml) French vermouth, 1 dash absinthe, and 2 dashes grenadine, garnished with a squeeze of lemon peel over the top.

The same hotel also offered the **Savoy Hotel Special Cocktail (No. 2)**, which shook 2 oz. (60 ml) Plymouth gin, 1 oz. (30 ml) French vermouth, and 2 dashes Dubonnet, garnished with a squeeze of orange peel over the top.

THE MONTGOMERY

ATTRIBUTED TO AUTHOR ERNEST HEMINGWAY

Stir
2 oz. (60 ml) dry gin
1 splash (5 ml) French vermouth

Since it all began, the preferred ratio of gin to vermouth in a Martini has seismically shifted. Victorian Martini aficionados ordered an equal balance of gin and Italian dry vermouth topped with a dash of orange bitters. At the turn of the century, the Martini went dry when extra-dry vermouth (and French vermouth) replaced sweet Italian vermouth. During the Depression, the 2:1 Martini lost its orange bitters. Then at the start of the Second World War, the super-dry Martini emerged. Author Ernest Hemingway called it a Montgomery—a 15:1 super-dry Martini. In his 1950 novel *Across the River and into the Trees* he aptly described this metamorphosis:

> "Two very dry Martinis," [Colonel Cantwell] said. "Montgomerys. Fifteen to one."
> The waiter who had been in the desert, smiled and was gone . . .

Hemingway named the variation after Field Marshal Bernard Law Montgomery, leader of the British Eighth Army during the Second World War's North African campaigns. The story goes that Monty would attack German field marshal Erwin Rommel—the Desert Fox—and his men only if His Majesty's forces outnumbered this formidable foe by a 15:1 ratio.

The Montgomery was actually a sign of the times. So was the story about British prime minister Winston Churchill waving a bottle of vermouth over his cocktail shaker and/or bowing toward France while making a Martini. There are some modern Martini drinkers who prefer an

One explanation for increasingly drier Martinis, from our friend Robert Hess who is at this moment probably stirring a round of Fitty-Fittys for himself and his new bride, Audrey, in Seattle: "If you look at all of the quotes about the various 'gymnastics' people go through to make their Dry Martini you'll notice that virtually to a one, the person attributed to this process was either a borderline or full-blown alcoholic. They would look at the gin (40 percent) then the vermouth (18 percent), and say 'Fie to you, vermouth!' because they wanted the full octane kick of the gin in their drink without any lesser strength product getting in their way."

During the 1930s and 1940s, a **Medium Martini** combined 2 oz. (60 ml) gin and 1 oz. (30 ml) each of both French and Italian vermouth.

Patrons of the Nassau Gun Club liked their **Perfect Martini** blended according to a truly classic formula: 4 oz. (120 ml) gin, 1 oz. (30 ml) each of both French and Italian vermouth, and 1 dash Bogart's orange bitters. More daring drinkers ordered a **Pall Mall Cocktail**, adding 1 tsp. white crème de menthe to the shaker.

The **Boomerang Cocktail** also made its way around parties, mixing 1 oz. (30 ml) gin, 1 oz. (30 ml) French vermouth, 1 oz. (30 ml) Italian vermouth, 1 dash Angostura bitters, and a maraschino cherry garnish.

According to gin expert Simon Ford, who got this straight from Winston Churchill's granddaughter, he never bowed toward France and omitted vermouth in his Martinis.

even drier blend: or "only the shadow of the vermouth bottle" or a quick spritz of vermouth. Remember, if you're going to fill a perfume or cologne atomizer with vermouth make sure it's clean—after all, you don't want to go down in history as the inventor of the Calvin Klein's Obsession Martini, do you?

What really happened? The Second World War struck a particular blow to vermouths and just about any liqueurs, apéritifs, or spirits produced in France or Italy. The pro-Nazi Vichy government in France banned the production of alcoholic beverages in 1940, except for spirits manufactured for export. The next year, the officials banned production altogether. The vermouth was gone. The pro-Nazi Italian government led by Benito Mussolini wasn't helping vermouth exportation to Allied nations like the United States and Britain. The vermouth was really gone. (What can you say? Hitler was not only a vegetarian, he was a teetotaler and liked his colleagues to follow his path.)

By the time world peace was once again restored, numerous veteran bartenders who knew how to use and store vermouths had died in battle. There weren't enough masters to mentor the new generation of bartenders who came of age during the 1950s. For the Martini, the vermouth was almost forever gone.

THE REVERSE MARTINI
ATTRIBUTED TO CHEF JULIA CHILD

She dropped a raw chicken on American television, picked it up, and continued cooking with the sort of panache that few people have the confidence to acquire. She introduced the American public to the joys of French cuisine at home. Chef Julia Child was larger than life.

When she and her husband, Paul, moved to Paris, in 1948, she found herself enthralled with the cuisine, enrolled in Le Cordon Bleu, and began teaching American women in France how to cook true French food. The rest is culinary history.

But we want to talk about a drink that she savored in between bottles of the finest wines—the Reverse Martini. Seems that her husband fancied himself an amateur mixologist. He entertained guests such as chef Jacques Pépin with a round of Reverse Martinis—his take on the French call for a Martini-Gin: sweet Italian vermouth served with a splash of gin on top.

Paul expanded his repertoire by making Reverse Manhattans with bourbon. And for his loving spouse, he continued to make Reverse Martinis (aka: Upside Down Martinis), which are still the finest accompaniment to fresh oysters, fish, and just about any light meat dish in the universe.

Jared has a more personal take on the story of this marvelous apéritif:

> If you're not the most famous authors at a book convention, you can only hope to have the booth next to the most famous ones. There we were, planted next to Julia Child and Jacques Pépin for an entire day, with their press line

Stir

0.25 oz. (10 ml) Beefeater London Dry Gin

1.5 oz. (45 ml) Noilly Prat dry vermouth

lemon twist

Prefer a Nosbig? Garnish your Initram with an onion.

—Jared Brown

. . . Of cognac, absinthe and vermouth. The use of the latter stimulant is fearfully injurious to mind, body and morals.

—*The Sunday Critic*, Logansport, Indiana (July 12, 1885)

The first time I tasted vermouth in a Martini, I thought my jaw was going to permanently lock in position. Acidic as vinegar. Nasty. In fact, it tasted worse—like vinegar with a touch of drain cleaner. I discovered nearly thirty years later that I wasn't far from wrong.

See, when all you have to test drive your first Martini is a dusty bottle of French vermouth that's been sitting in your dad's liquor cabinet for at least five years, you don't get the joy of mixing a Martini with even a whisper of the stuff.

It wasn't until I bought my first fresh bottle, cracked it open, and sampled a splash that I discovered this stuff was the missing link in my favorite drink.

When we moved back to New York in 2000, we were lucky enough to acquire more than a few miniatures of extra-dry vermouth. Straight into the vegetable crisper they went.

Every time we wanted to mix Martinis, we cracked open a fresh bottle that contained enough to make a Reverse Martini.

—Anistatia Miller

snaking through our stand. Occasionally, they needed a break and ducked out the back. We couldn't resist joining them.

Julia was wonderful, and had graciously forgotten the first time we met, when I mistook her for Dan Akyord dressed up as her (I'd been a desk clerk at the Essex House, he usually came in wearing disguises, and I loved his Julia Child skit; when she arrived I stuck her in his favorite suite and knew I'd got it wrong when she returned to the desk and said, "There must be some mistake, I was only booked for a regular room"—words Dan would never have said).

Anyway, she told us about her favorite Martini, a Reverse Martini with five parts Noilly Prat to one part London dry gin, built in an ice-filled wine goblet, optionally garnished with a twist. She went so far as to say there are few wines as good against firm, white-fleshed fish such as swordfish or halibut.

Back in 1957, an American diplomat assigned to Jidda (where he had to drink with the blinds drawn) mixed his **Diplomatic Martini**, stirring 1 oz. (30 ml) dry vermouth to 1 tsp. (5 ml) dry gin. He swore, "I'm going to stretch my bottle of gin until I'm relieved of this post."

Philip Harding, who in the 1960s created the first syndicated wine column, answered a request from "A.L. in San Francisco" for a low-alcohol cocktail with a **Reverse Martini**, stirring 2 oz. (60 ml) dry vermouth over ice with 0.5 oz. (15 ml) dry gin floated on top.

It was reported in 1953 that a group of French producers at a party in New York deemed that a better **French Reverse Martini** could be made by stirring 0.5 oz. (15 ml) cognac with 2 oz. (60 ml) dry gin.

THE BERLIN STATION CHIEF

CREATED BY JEFFREY CARLISLE & CHARLES WHARTON

How far can you go with super-dry and still have a fine Martini? Inspiration can be divined from recent literary sources. Carlisle and Wharton of the Policy Hut in Washington, D.C., created a sophisticated Martini made with single malt whiskey instead of vermouth. Their recipe was based on a passage from Norman Mailer's 1991 novel *Harlot's Ghost*:

> [William King Harvey] mixed a batch of Martinis: He filled the shaker with ice, poured in a quarter inch of scotch, poured it out, then loaded the pitcher with gin … "The scotch adds that no-see-um flannel taste you're looking for. Slips the job down your gullet" [he commented]. He drank off his first fill, gave his glass another, and passed me one. It did slide down. Smooth fire, sweet ice. I had the disconnected thought that if I ever wrote a novel I would call it Smooth Fire, Sweet Ice.

A **Golden Triangle Station Chief** uses a blended scotch like Chivas Regal, Glenlivet, Glenfiddich.

A **Paraguay Station Chief** uses Bombay Original Dry Gin rather than Bombay Sapphire.

A 1930s **Paisley Cocktail** stirred up 2 oz. (60 ml) dry gin, 0.5 oz. (15 ml) French vermouth, and 1 tsp. (5 ml) blended Scotch whiskey, garnished with a lemon peel.

The **Royal Wedding** served at Oliver's at the Mayflower Park Hotel in Seattle shook 2 oz. (60 ml) Stolichnaya vodka in a shaker rinsed with 0.5 oz. Chivas Regal 12-Year, garnished with a lemon twist.

Shake
2 oz. (60 ml) Bombay Sapphire Gin
0.5 oz. (15 ml) Lagavulin

lemon twist

Pour the scotch over the ice, swirl to coat, and then toss it out. Add the gin and shake. Rub the twist around the bottom of the glass. Strain and pour the mix. Let stand for a few seconds, and then discard the peel.

Some other great whiskies to try include: Macallan, Ardbeg, Bruchladdich, Bunnahabhain, and Laphroaig.

I should never have switched from scotch to Martinis.

—regarded as Humphrey Bogart's last words

THE VIRGIN MARTINI

Shake

3 drops Angostura bitters

3 stuffed green olives or lemon twist

You can avoid tennis elbow from excessive shaking if you add 2 oz. (60 ml) mineral water, lemon-lime soda, or lemonade.

For a **Super-Dry Virgin Martini**, wave the vermouth bottle over the mixing glass, then do the same with the gin bottle.

It was summer, and we were on our way to attend a wedding ceremony at the Bogus Basin ski resort near Boise, Idaho. After renting a four-wheel drive at the airport, we stopped off to fortify the passengers for the long, twenty-mile drive up that the rental agent had cautioned was winding, steep, and boring. It was Friday night at the local hotel lounge, but we managed to squeeze onto a few barstools.

We were on our second round (everyone except our designated driver), when a very pretty—but obviously underage—young woman wandered up to the bar. The bartender offered her a Virgin Martini. It certainly got our attention!

He placed a cocktail glass filled with ice and water on the bar to chill, then spilled it out. He dropped two olives into the glass, wrung out a lemon twist over the top, and discarded the rind. Then he filled a shaker with ice, affixed the lid, and began to shake. He shook, and shook, and shook. Finally, he poured the contents into the glass and slid it across the bar to the girl. "Now drink it in good health," he said with a wink to us, "and come back in a few years."

But seriously. Since so much of what makes up a Martini is the show of meticulous preparation, a Virgin Martini is not completely impossible. The right glass, proper service, and the right garnish is all it takes.

If you're not pouring the VM's main ingredient (water) out of liquor bottles, try to come up with some decent glass or crystal decanters to set the stage.

After all, so much of the Martini's appeal is its inherent romance; the alcohol is almost secondary. Also, make sure whoever is bartending wipes the rim of each glass with a lemon twist: a trick we learned from a bartender who made nearly Virgin Martinis himself.

Bitters? In a Virgin Martini? In any Martini? Obviously, most early Martini recipes contained bitters. Angostura bitters, the best known of all, was invented in 1824 by a Prussian army surgeon who'd gone to Venezuela to join Simon Bolivar's forces in the liberation of South America. Created in the town of Angostura, his gentian root concoction still bears its name.

We recently went to buy a bottle of Angostura bitters. (No, we didn't finish ours, we'd misplaced it.) We wandered up and down the supermarket aisles before we gave up and asked the manager. He led us to the check-out counter, opened a locked cabinet, and pulled out a bottle. When we asked why he kept them hidden, he explained that people had been taking them off the shelves, gulping them down (after all, it is 90 proof), and leaving the empties behind. Have you ever tasted straight bitters? These people should have been easy to spot: writhing across the floor with their faces sucked in so far they could hide behind a dime. We asked if he had the same trouble with Chinese cooking wine (grain alcohol, water, and a little salt). No one ever touched it. Go figure.

Did you hear the one about the couple who'd been together so long they were on their second bottle of bitters? It's been 20 years and we're on our 300th bottle.

—Anistatia Miller

Trying to explain the meaning of the word "oxymoron"? Virgin Martini is not a bad place to start.

THE BOTTOM LINE ON GIN MARTINIS

A DUBIOUS HONOR

There are few moments in this world, especially ours, when you feel honored to be thrown out of a bar. It happened to us in the 1990s when we went to visit a grotto of the Dry Martini—the Persian Aub Zam Zam.

You'd reckon that a little hole-in-the-wall place in the Haight-Ashbury district of San Francisco would be a bastion of the vaunted Dry Martini. Yet, when we walked in and sat at the bar, owner Bruno Mooshei, whose dad had opened the place in 1941, was more subjective about the Dry Martini that anyone else on the planet.

We didn't know that he made a Dry Martini only with Boord's gin and Boissiere vermouth in a 1000:1 ratio, served in a 3 oz. glass.

When we asked for a 3:1 made with Plymouth gin, all he said was: "You see the door? It's your door!"

—Anistatia Miller

We can't tell you how many times some one has come up to us and yelped, "That's not a Martini!" We got a little paranoid until we read Jack Townsend's 1951 tome *The Bartender's Book*. President of the Bartender's Union of New York, Townsend devoted an entire chapter to Martinis with the catchy title "The Martini Family." This well-seasoned author made a very valid claim at the onset: "One thing that sets a Martini aside from all other drinks is the fact that any real deviation from accepted formula is classified under another name."

After citing dozens of examples, Townsend provided his recipes for the Martini, Dry Martini, Perfect, Sweet Martini, Cooperstown, Turf, Parisian, Cardinale, Army, Society, Torpedo, Allies, Fourth Estate, Lone Tree, Bronx, and Gibson.

We have to admit, the Gin Martini family is pretty awesome. Yet, we still have to pay credance to the fact that no one agrees on how the Silver Bullet should be made. So we asked a few of our friends for their opinions.

We asked Sasha Petraske of Milk & Honey and Dutch Kills his take on the Martini. He gave it to us with both barrels, standing up for purity and perfection:

> Certainly my favorite proportion is 2:1, assuming that it's 86 proof gin. Olives are my preference, if they are delicious, but if it's a rubbery Manzanilla "bar olive," my go-to alternate is a Martini "On Toast" (read: burned lemon peel garnish).

We agree on the whole that if you choose the path of the true Martini, you need to be very exacting in your portions, and your selection of spirit, vermouth, and garnish. Yet, can everyone aspire to this passion?

A legend in his own time, master London mixologist Dick Bradsell takes a different, even more classic approach to this very subjective subject:

> It used to be that a customer came in and told you how to make his Martini. At the Zanzibar Club, I was trained for a year by my mentor Ray Cook to make the regulars Martinis just how they liked them. It was because Ray was leaving to be a puppeteer. Mr T ... had a 20:1 Tanqueray Export, Noilly Prat on the rocks in a whiskey glass with an olive. Mr J: I had his Booth's and Martini Dry very dry and straight up with an ultrathin twist of lemon peel sprayed and wiped, etc.
>
> When Ray left, they just stopped drinking them, looked grumpy, and went elsewhere for their excellence. In some ways it's all about perception. They didn't want some smart arse kid making their sacred beauties. It couldn't be that easy, could it?
>
> Well, it is. Simplest drink in the book. Almost any idiot can make one (including me when I'm drunk, for instance) but it's making it well.
>
> So all ladies and gentlemen should have their call "a 5:1 Bombay Dry with Noilly and two olives" would be mine. Please don't fart about doing it weird or fancy pants, traditional will suffice. And please serve it quickly very, very cold (and drink it whilst it's smiling at you).

Thanks, Dick. We bow to your sage words of wisdom.

Jack Townsend's version of the **Cooperstown** shook 1 oz. (30 ml) dry gin, 0.5 oz. (15 ml) French vermouth, 0.5 oz. (15 ml) Italian vermouth, and two sprigs of fresh mint.

Townsend's version of the **Cardinale** shook 1 oz. (30 ml) dry gin, 0.5 oz. (15 ml) French vermouth, 0.5 oz. (15 ml) Italian vermouth, and 1 dash Campari.

FROM RUSSIA WITH LOVE
CLASSIC VODKA MARTINIS

Russia and Poland are not the cheeriest of places during the bleak winter months. Before central heating, electric lighting, and other mod-cons you can well imagine life was even darker during the Dark Ages. Beer made it a little more bearable. As Prince Vladimir of Kiev was quoted as saying in the 1113 A.D. tome *The Russian Primary Chronicle*:

> Russians are merrier drinking—without it they cannot live.

The dramatic portrayal of vodka's birth and rise to international prominence has an impressive cast of characters. The curtain opens. We begin.

The Polish court loved the Asian import called arrack and learned how to distill spirits from the Genoese merchants who had settled there. They started making their own liquor from grain. The 1405 court records of the Świętokrzyskie Voivodship mention this new potable. But it still wasn't called vodka.

When the Genoese passed through Russia, in 1426, Grand Prince Vasily III was more than delighted to receive a gift of this same imported spirit.

FATIMA BLUSH:
I made you all wet.
JAMES BOND:
Yes, but my Martini is still dry.

—*Never Say Never Again*
(1983)

Some great European vodkas to try include: Stolichnaya, Luksusowa, Moskovskaya, Beluga, Russian Standard, Absolut, Ketel One, Wyborowa Exquisite, Chopin, Sipsmith Barley, and Belvedere.

Of the New World vodkas, Charbay gets our vote.

Within a few years, monasteries were ordered to distill a grain-based version called "bread wine."

Polish pharmacist Stefan Falimirz wrote a book of medical treatments in 1534 titled *O ziolach i o mocy ich* [On Herbs and Their Potency], in which the term "*wodka*" first appeared in print. The prolific chemist detailed the preparation of more than seventy vodka-based elixirs.

Vodka was rectified with herbs and spices that were guaranteed to cure everything from warts and lost love to menstrual cramps and hair loss. He also offered a few tips on how to smoke vodka over alder or other aromatic woods to impart a pleasant character. (Actually, smoking the vodka got rid of the sour, sometimes rotten aroma that these early vodkas possessed.)

Yeah, vodka was pretty rough stuff in those days. Made by commercial producers or by home distillers from bread, grain, milk, what have you, this spirit was anything but smooth. Emperor Peter the Great had cracked down on home-brewed vodka by mandating liquor licenses to limit sales. Reportedly a two-liter per day vodka drinker, he obviously had tried some moonshiner's outlay and hated it.

Enter German chemist Johann Tobias Lowitz, who toyed around with activated charcoal. He discovered, in 1785, that the stuff removed noxious odors, such as the smell of sick people, putrid meats, and rotting vegetables. Taking a teaching post at the St. Petersburg Academy of Sciences in 1793, Lowitz became obsessed with filtering all sorts of things through different types of charcoal. Within three years he successfully collected pure ethyl alcohol by filtering it through hardwood charcoal that was activated to increase its adsorption of unsightly particles and offensive aromas. Certainly Empress Catherine the Great must have been pretty pleased with these findings. She made it illegal for anyone other than the aristocracy to purvey vodka altogether. Talk about keeping a secret to yourself!

Enter Ivan Smirnov, who opened a distillery in 1815, producing eaux-de-vie and vodka in a warehouse that was part of the remains of the Wine Court, demolished during the War of 1812. His vodka earned him enough to register the company and build a new distillery near the Iron Bridge. His son Pyotr took over the burgeoning business in 1873 when Ivan died.

Being at the right place at the right time is everything. The Smirnovs were no exception. Continuous distillation, invented in 1823, made it possible to make barrel loads of spirit that had a softer character than pot-stilled distillates. Lowitz's charcoal filtration method upped the ante by cleaning the spirit to a remarkable smoothness thanks to the use of birchwood charcoal.

Together, technological advances brought Smirnov's vodka not only public admiration, but Emperor Alexander III also appointed the house a royal warrant in 1886. (This was quite a coup: The czar's annual vodka consumption totaled up to more rubles than his Fabergé egg purchases!)

Things went pretty well for the Smirnovs and their vodka until Pyotr passed away, in 1898, followed by his widow the following year, leaving their sons Sergei, Alexey, Pyotr, Nikolai, and Vladimir to run the shop. Everyone but Pyotr sold their rights by the time Tsar Nikolai II nationalized the empire's vodka industry in 1904, yet he continued to manage the distillery until he died in 1910.

In Poland, it is customary to serve vodka in small shot glasses. This, in view of their drinking customs, is more merciful than stingy. Pouring yourself a drink and drinking it is simply not the norm when amongst friends. A round should be poured for all, glasses raised, toast made, and drinks drained, then repeated as soon as someone else thinks another drink would be a good idea.

BEEFSTEAK MARTINI

Practically a Bloody Mary, we created the **Beefsteak Martini**, in 2000, to match up to a good steak. Serving prime rib or a nice sirloin? This will give the best red wine a run for its money.

Place a colander over a bowl. Fill it with coarsely chopped beefsteak tomatoes. Put a few small plates or other heavy crockery on top of the tomatoes to press them gently and leave the whole mess to sit for a few hours. A light pink and fairly clear liquid will drain out from the tomatoes. Bottle this and stick it in the refrigerator. Once it's chilled, you're ready to mix.

Stir 1.5 oz. (45ml) Beefeater gin, 1 oz. (30 ml) tomato water, 0.75 oz. (20 ml) dry vermouth, and two dashes of Tabasco sauce over ice in a mixing glass for half the usual time—about 10 seconds. Strain into a chilled cocktail glass. Garnish with a blue-cheese-stuffed cherry tomato.

His widow Eugenia kept the business running until a few months before the 1917 October Revolution, when the distillery was confiscated and placed under state control. Luck had it that Eugenia had already remarried and moved to Italy with her diplomat husband. She later moved to Nice, France. Vladimir also made his escape to France but not until he fled to the Ukraine, where he was captured by Revolutionary guards. Being in cahoots with the White Army and a former imperial purveyor didn't help his case. He was put in front of a firing squad four times before the White Army helped him escape to Turkey, where, in 1920, he opened a distillery before heading to Paris with some of his wares.

There were loads of Russian expats living in the City of Light who hankered for vodka. Smirnov changed the spelling of his name and hawked Smirnoff vodka at the New York Bar on Rue Daunou and at Henry's Bar around the corner on Rue de Volney.

But in wine- and pastis-centric France, Smirnoff failed miserably at convincing the locals to drink vodka, despite Pete Petiot's efforts to introduce a simple drink like the Bloody Mary at the New York Bar. The French had no desire to associate, even on a social level, with a spirit that reminded them about heated political issues such as communism. "Pastis time" debates were enough for them. The only people who bought vodka were homesick Russian exiles and other East European expats.

Nearly a decade later, the despondent Smirnoff was still living in Paris when he befriended a naturalized Ukrainian-American visitor named Rudolph Kunett. Vodka was "mother's milk" to the young entrepreneur, who was willing to bet on the spirit's success in the American market based on his nostalgic appreciation and the post-Repeal emergence of the cocktail trade.

He purchased the United States rights to both Smirnoff's recipe and brand name. That same year, Kunett opened the American Smirnoff Distillery in Bethel, Connecticut. But he forgot something. Isolationist America wasn't quick to embrace foreign products. Just like Cynar, vodka was not something the average American drank. (Haven't tried Cynar? It's an Italian artichoke-flavored aperitif.)

Though his hopes were buoyed by the Russian government's all-out 1930s push to launch Russian vodka in the United States as the post-Prohibition spirit of choice, which sold out the stock in liquor stores, he still struggled.

Enter John G. Martin, the president of G. F. Heublein Brothers, Inc. This marketer was raring to get back to the company's heyday, when it imported vermouth and produced premixed Heublein Club Cocktails, including Martinis. He sensed that Kunett's problem wasn't the product's quality, it was a lack of marketing muscle. So, in 1939, Kunett sold his interests to Martin for $14,000. He still had faith, taking on a management position.

Enter John A. Morgan, who loved the ginger beer that came from his homeland—Britain. After returning from a trip back home, he put it upon himself to introduce the drink to the United States. Packaged in crockery bottles emblazoned with his Hollywood restaurant's name—Cock 'n' Bull—Morgan produced his first load. He arrived in New York, where he met his friends Martin and Kunett at the Chatham Hotel Bar, in 1941. The Moscow Mule was born.

We can't help wondering if the inventors of the Moscow Mule had the same 1926 copy of *The Cocktail Book: A Sideboard Manual for Gentlemen* that we have. In it, in the one section where readers of books on drink rarely tread—the non-alcoholic drinks chapter—there is a Mule's Collar recipe: "Use a large glass. Juice of one lime; one dash Angostura bitters; three lumps ice; one bottle dry ginger ale."

Whether or not they took their inspiration from this obscure source, we discovered something wonderful. Angostura bitters is delicious in a Moscow Mule. Try adding a dash to your next one.

A perfectionist once asked if he could chill a Martini with liquid nitrogen. It reminded us of this passage from Martin Cruz Smith's 1989 novel **Polar Star**:

"The year before, an Intourist guide had taken a group of Americans into the [Siberian] taiga and laid out an even more splendid lunch but had forgotten to turn the [vodka] bottle.

"After many toasts with warm tea . . . the guide poured glasses of nearly frozen almost congealed vodka and showed his guests how to drink it in one go. 'Like this,' he said. He tipped the glass, drank it, and fell over dead. What the guide had forgotten was that Siberian vodka was nearly two hundred proof, almost pure alcohol, and would still flow at a temperature that would freeze the gullet and stop the heart like a sword. Just the shock was enough to kill him. It was sad, of course, but it was also hilarious. Imagine the poor Americans sitting around the campfire, looking at their Russian guide and saying, 'This is a Siberian picnic.'"

The three friends chipped in to purchase five hundred copper mugs embossed with "Little Moscow" and awaited the delivery of cases of ginger beer. When it arrived, the '21' Club, the Waldorf-Astoria Hotel, and the Sherry-Netherland Hotel all gave the drink an enthusiastic reception. Morgan's ginger beer project went on hiatus when the United States entered World War II and he served in the military. It never really gained a second wind when he returned. But Kunett's and Martin's vodka continued its entry into the cocktail lexicon, picking up momentum immediately after the war thanks to a first-time novelist.

Former British intelligence agent and journalist Ian Fleming published his first novel—*Casino Royale*—in 1953. He'd borrowed the main character's name—James Bond—from the author of the 1936 book *Birds of the West Indies*. He assigned the secret agent some of his own personal tastes for women, food, and Martinis—Vodka Martinis. During the Second World War, Fleming lamented the slump in quality at his favorite London watering hole, the American Bar at the Savoy Hotel:

SHAKEN NOT STIRRED

When I tell you that the Savoy Hotel are [*sic*] now mixing Martinis out of bath-tub gin and sherry you will know that we are rapidly progressing back to swamp life and the transitional period is distasteful.

Q: Should you eat the olive first or last?

A: First. It's not healthy to drink on an empty stomach.

Fleming's James Bond thrillers were immediate best sellers throughout the Cold War. And Bond's Martini preferences became the universal icon of sophistication, especially in the wake of the 1960s blockbuster motion pictures.

During President Jimmy Carter's term in office, the three-Martini lunch was viewed as a negative perk; a devious tax deduction taken by fat-cat corporate types. Something had to be at fault. The nation was in the midst of a severe recession as the 1970s progressed. Cocktails were out and frozen fruit drinks, wines, and beer were in.

Gin and vodka joined scotch and whiskey as "establishment" beverages, consumed by straight-laced corpies in Martinis and Manhattans. The hip, leisure-suit and disco-dress crowd sipped on Screwdrivers, Capecodders, and Piña Coladas along with strawberry wine, rosé wine, chablis, and lager.

The fact that vodka made the perfect pairing for cranberry juice, cola, orange juice, and soda led, in 1975, to vodka replacing scotch as America's best-selling spirit.

We'll continue with our story of vodka's rise in a bit. But we want to focus on Vodka Martinis for now. They may not have the lineage of their gin siblings, but they did establish a new generation of Martini drinkers who demanded just as much sophistication as their predecessors.

DEMPSEY COCKTAIL

REPORTEDLY CREATED IN DEAUVILLE, FRANCE

Stir

1 oz. (30 ml) Smirnoff vodka

1 oz. (30 ml) Noilly Prat vermouth

1 oz. (30 ml) bourbon or rye whiskey

lemon twist

During his visits, King Alphonse of Spain drove people to drink in Deauville. When he arrived for breakfast, everyone stood silently. When he'd sat down and drunk "his morning cocktail" everyone would order whatever he'd had. After one Sunday when his sudden taste for a Gin Fizz wiped out all the Hollands stocks in town (and more had to be flown in from Brussels, as Paris was *en vacance*), the waiters advised his majesty's staff of which drinks were best stocked and made sure he ordered those.

The "bathing capital of France" was what American journalists during the 1920s called Deauville. It seems an unlikely spot to find vodka being shaken or stirred. Yet one intrepid reporter thought it was worth a mention.

Amid the notes about nouveau-riche American women sporting the latest skin-tight bathing suits, there were reports of Reginald Vanderbilt throwing great parties onboard his yacht *Maud* and the Duchess of Talleyrand (formerly Anna Gould) showing off her latest Callot gown. Five casinos kept husbands occupied at baccarat tables, including one "grandson of a famous dry goods merchant of New York and Philadelphia" who denied losing 800,000 francs in a single session. "He says it may have been as much as 8,000 but he does not remember," the journalist noted.

He further conjectured that this memory loss could easily have occurred "as they sell the Dempsey Cocktail here in all the resorts for millionaires. They are made of Russian vodka, French vermouth, and American whiskey and get the name Dempsey from the fact that the fourth one is guaranteed to knock out the toughest of the high rollers."

All of Paris goes *en vacance* during August, heading to the beaches in droves.

Did Russian expat Vladimir Smirnoff follow the migration to Deauville and sell a few cases of vodka before the reporter and his millionaire quarry arrived for the season? Maybe. What we do know is that this is the first mention in print of vodka meeting dry vermouth.

So, there it is. Before vodka found its way into the Martini, before it was poured into a Bloody Mary, it was getting mixed into American tourists' cocktails by French bartenders.

Another drink named in honor of heavyweight boxing champ Jack Dempsey during the 1920s also hit Deauville's beaches. **The Dempsey** was made with 1 oz. (30 ml) dry gin, 2 oz. (60 ml) calvados, 1 tsp. grenadine, and 2 dashes absinthe. Maybe the vodka ran out.

Yes, wealthy Americans escaped Prohibition with extended European holidays. But where? In August, they descended on Deauville. Starting in 1921, it was reported they outnumbered all other foreign nationalities there and set the tone with their demands for cocktails and jazz bands.

IRON CURTAIN COCKTAIL

CREATED BY GUS ERENGERTH AT THE UNITED NATIONS DELEGATES LOUNGE

Stir

2 oz. (60 ml) Smirnoff vodka

0.25 oz. (15 ml) Noilly Prat vermouth

lemon twist

In the 1937 British cocktail compendium the *Café Royal Cocktail Book*, William J. Tarling documented a vodka cocktail by London barman H. Parker called the **Devil's Torch**, shaking 1.5 oz. (45 ml) Russian vodka, 1.5 oz. (45 ml) French vermouth, and 3 dashes grenadine.

In the same book, **Godfrey's Corpse Reviver**, by Godfrey Baldini, shook 1.5 oz. (45 ml) dry gin, 0.75 oz. (20 ml) Russian vodka, 1 dash grenadine, and 1 dash Angostura bitters. And P. Silvani's **Green Park Cocktail** shook 1 oz. (30 ml) Seagers gin, 1 oz. (30 ml) Latvian rye vodka, 0.5 oz. (15 ml) Cointreau, and 0.5 oz. (15 ml) fresh grapefruit juice.

Lake Success, New York, may seem an unlikely place for a Martini to be invented, but it was. Situated in northwest Long Island, this little village was home to the Sperry Gyroscope Company, makers of military and naval equipment. The place was hopping during the Second World War when the plant employed twenty-two thousand workers. Then, in 1946, peacetime returned. Part of the property was transformed into the United Nations while its Manhattan headquarters were under construction.

A lounge was installed to quench the thirsts of the delegates who represented the General Assembly's fifty-one member nations. Diplomats filed in, beginning at 10:30 a.m. to guzzle fresh-squeezed orange juice—thirty to forty gallons a day. Things changed at 5:30 p.m. That's when Norwegian expat Gus Erengerth took his place behind the bar, crafting such potent potions as the Iron Curtain Cocktail.

When Britain's Princess Elizabeth was preparing for her wedding, in 1947, to Lieutenant Philip Mountbatten, a British delegate asked Gus to create a Lilibet Special (that was the future queen's childhood nickname). The Norwegian blended gin and Metaxa brandy with lime juice and a touch of Drambuie.

It appears vodka first usurped gin as vermouth's cocktail-glass dancing partner out of necessity, not preference, in some circles. During World War II, soldiers fighting abroad—and the inevitable pack of journalists who trailed along—mixed cocktails with whatever ingredients were at hand.

SHAKEN NOT STIRRED

While stationed in Russia, in 1943, Associated Press journalist Henry Clarence Cassidy recalled: "The cocktails were seven parts vodka to one part Persian vermouth from a precious bottle [writer] Walter Kerr brought from Tehran."

Another war correspondent, Quentin James Reynolds, was a little more opinionated about his experience, recalling in 1944: "As far as our troops everywhere are concerned, beer is the aristocrat of all drinks. The staple drink in Iran is a concoction called V and V. It is half Persian vodka and half Persian vermouth, and it tastes like liquid soap."

The earliest recorded combination of vodka and vermouth comes from Persia. Yes, Persia! In 1933, the Hittite Cocktail was announced from Tehran as "a drink unknown even to the most exclusive New York speakeasies." It contained equal parts Russian vodka, Italian vermouth, and water. (This is about the standard dilution for a Martini.) The name comes from a humorous claim that the recipe was discovered in cuneiform on a small clay tablet dating back to the Hittites, circa 1500 B.C. The great irony: by spuriously claiming the drink's ancient origins they actually got it in print for the first time. (Note: In case you missed it above, they were not serious about finding the ancient recipe . . . or were they?)

Russia had its own Prohibition, from 1914 to 1923. It inspired England to consider passing a similar law, which nearly happened in 1915.

During one of his many journeys during the 1920s and 1930s to search for a good drink, journalist Charles H. Baker Jr. discovered that American troops stationed in Siberia during the First World War warmed themselves with **The Vladivostok Virgin**, shaking 1.5 oz. (45 ml) Russian vodka, 1.5 oz. (45 ml) dry gin, 1 oz. (30 ml) unsweetened grapefruit juice, and 1 dash Angostura bitters, garnished with a paper-thin slice of cucumber.

The Hittite Cocktail from the 1930s shook 1 oz. (30 ml) Russian vodka, 1 oz. (30 ml) Italian vermouth, 1 oz. (30 ml) bottled water.

Miguel Boadas at Barcelona's temple of cocktail, Bar Boadas, crafted a **Beso de Cosaco**, throwing 1 oz. (30 ml) dry gin, 1 oz. (30 ml) vodka, 1 oz. (30 ml) French vermouth, 1 dash Picón, and 1 dash curaçao in the classic Cuban/Catalan style of mixing (for an example see illustration on page 126), garnished with a Griottine cherry.

The year is 1934. Vodka crashed onto American shores. The Russians saw an opportunity to capitalize on the repeal of Prohibition and began throwing zakuski parties in Washington, D.C., as well as events in New York and other cities, with reports of liquor stores selling out of this new novelty.

The Russian embassy in the nation's capital helped boost sales. One news piece from Washington, D.C., headlined "Vodka's The Smart Drink," commented that "Russians are shrewd. Local liquor stores sold out of vodka soon after the Russian embassy's big reception. Vodka has become the 'smart' drink, and such a large clientele is assured for that Soviet export that the party was an excellent commercial investment."

That same year, Victor of New York's St. Moritz Hotel on Central Park South made a name for himself and his S.O.S., which he made with three parts vodka, one part French vermouth, two spoonsful of crème de mandarin, a dash of absinthe, and a dash of Angostura bitters. But he wasn't the only St. Moritz bartender mixing drinks that could easily be mistaken for Vodka Martinis. (The St. Moritz was the site of at least one vodka-themed cocktail party the next year as well.)

That September, at the Waldorf-Astoria, bartenders pitted their mixing talents against each other in what was probably the first American vodka cocktail competition. While the band played "The Russian Boat Song," Frank Pramaggoni of the St. Moritz took first prize with a drink made up of three parts Russian vodka, one part French vermouth, served in a glass flavored with dashes of Angostura bitters and a few drops of grenadine. It was the first Vodka Martini.

We know about cocktail competitions. Jared's got a story to tell about one of them:

> We'd tasted our way through ten Martinis, judging the 1996 Seattle Martini Competition. At the after party, there were more drinks and, thankfully, nibbles at the Mayflower Park Hotel.
>
> I can remember the woman only as Mrs. Robinson (not her name, but she was the epitome of Anne Bancroft in a little black dress). Perhaps we'd been talking. But I first noticed her when she whisked me across the room to the pianist.
>
> "Play us a tango, darling!" she said as much to his surprise as mine.
>
> No one was dancing and he'd stuck to Cole Porter, Fats Waller, and the like. There's no question who led as we cleared a length of the room. She even positioned me to dip her. Afterward, she purred, "Enough of this. Let's go upstairs."
>
> Anistatia, who'd been stifling a snicker at me the whole time, leaned in and said, "I'm afraid he's taken."
>
> "I saw him first, dear," Mrs. R. replied.
>
> Anistatia flashed her wedding band and said, "Perhaps, but I married him first."

The **S.O.S.** shook 1.5 oz. (45 ml) vodka, 0.5 oz. French vermouth, 2 tsp. crème de mandarin liqueur, 1 dash absinthe, and 1 dash Angostura bitters.

The St. Moritz Hotel's Frank Parmaggoni made a **Vodka Martini** that shook 1.5 oz. (45 ml) vodka and 0.5 oz. French vermouth, strained into a cocktail glass coated with 1 dash Angostura bitters and a few drops of grenadine syrup.

If stuffed green olives don't appeal to you, then try the **Buckeye**: Simply garnish a Vodka Martini with a black olive.

To make a **Boston Bullet**, simply garnish a Vodka Martini with an almond-stuffed green olive.

In London, during the 1930s, bartender Heini Schmidt concocted a **Lenna Cocktail**, stirring 1.5 oz. (45 ml) vodka, 1.5 oz. (45 ml) champagne, and 2 dashes of grenadine, garnished with a lemon twist.

At another 1930s London bar, "Fitz" Fitzgerald made his **Little Tickle Cocktail**, shaking 1.5 oz. (45 ml) Seagers gin, 0.75 oz. (20 ml) vodka, and 0.75 oz. (20 ml) crème yvette, garnished with a red cocktail cherry.

Even in the 1930s, London bartenders were divining blue drinks for the trend-conscious Bright Young Things. The **Nervo-Knox Cocktail** fit the bill to a tee, shaking 1 oz. (30 ml) vodka, 1 oz. (30 ml) blue curaçao, 0.5 oz. (15 ml) fresh lemon juice, and 0.5 oz. (15 ml) fresh lime juice.

BURNS STRAIGHT UP

ADAPTED FROM GEORGE BURNS'S RECIPE

Stir

2 oz. (60 ml) Smirnoff vodka

0.5 oz. (15 ml) Noilly Prat vermouth

olive

Make mine a Vodka Martini, straight up. Oh, and with an olive.

—George Burns, *18 Again*

Burns and Allen reputedly ended their comedy shows with the following lines:

GEORGE BURNS: "Say good night, Gracie."

GRACIE ALLEN: "Good night, Gracie."

We've been ending our speaking engagements with those same lines. Hopefully our union lasts as long as their thirty-eight-year marriage.

"People keep asking me, 'George, you are eighty-eight, how do you do it?' You make films, you do television, you give concerts, you record albums, smoke cigars, drink Martinis, go out with pretty girls. How do you do it? It's simple. For instance, a Martini. You fill the glass with ice; then pour in some gin and a touch of dry vermouth, add an olive, and you've got yourself a Martini."

At the age of ninety-three, Burns was asked if he felt like he was slowing up. He replied: "I've noticed a few signs, for instance . . . When I blow smoke rings I've noticed they're smaller and not as round as they used to be. And when I drink a Martini, instead of two olives, I'm down to one."

Burns considered his Vodka Martini as much a part of his daily ritual as playing cards, smoking cigars, exercising, and taking an afternoon nap. During his century-long life, Burns knew all the big show people: George Jessel (who allegedly invented the Bloody Mary because he hated the smell of potato vodka), Dean Martin (the "Martini Man"), and W. C. Fields (who drank two prebreakfast double Martinis daily).

One story goes that Burns ran into Fields after the famed lush was ordered to go on the wagon. Fields explained: "Well, George, my dear friend, your source is impeccable. It's quite true I'm not drinking anymore . . . However, I'm not drinking any less either."

Journalist Hugh Pickett recalled one backstage visit in 1986:

George was in his tux pants and his white shirt, making Martinis, and I can vouch for it, they were lethal. I had two, so did he, and then he went out and wowed a sold-out house, never missed a beat, or a step when he tap-danced.

There's something to be said for listening to what your body says that you can and cannot do. Moderation doesn't mean total abstinence, even as the years get shorter. It means taking what enjoyment you can from the things that you like and knowing when to put the glass down, stub out the cigar, drink a glass of water, brush your teeth, turn out the lights, get some sleep, oh yeah, and know that you can do it again tomorrow.

Our own **Lucky Martini** mixes 3 oz. (90 ml) vodka with 7 drops French vermouth. Stir gently 7 to 11 times in a clockwise direction. Garnish with 3 frozen gambling dice.

Dry Vodka Martinis may have been to George Burns's liking, but in London during the 1937 coronation of King George VI W. E. Edwards was serving a **Royal Toast Cocktail**, shaking 1 oz. (30 ml) vodka, 1 oz. (30 ml) cherry brandy, and 1 oz. (30 ml) Noilly Prat dry vermouth.

Happiness is a Dry Martini and a good woman . . . Or a bad woman.

—George Burns

THE VESPER

CREATED BY IAN FLEMING AND IVAR BRYCE

Shake

3 oz. (90 ml) Plymouth gin

1 oz. (30 ml) Moskovskaya vodka

0.5 oz. (15 ml) Kina Lillet

lemon peel

We served Vespers to our New Year's Eve guests in red wine goblets, which captured the drink's distinctive citrus edge, and made it tougher to spill (which they still managed to do after one or two).

"A dry martini," [Bond] said. "One. In a deep champagne goblet . . . Three measures of Gordon's, one of vodka, half a measure of Kina Lillet. Shake it very well until it's ice-cold, then add a large thin slice of lemon-peel. Got it?"

—*Casino Royale* (1953)

Just like his Victorian predecessor Sherlock Holmes, British superspy James Bond epitomized modern sophistication and savoir faire. A notorious liter-a-day vodka drinker himself, Bond's creator, Ian Fleming, introduced the character's impeccable taste in food and drink throughout the pages of his first thriller, *Casino Royale.*

During the Second World War, fellow Etonian and part owner of the North American Newspaper Alliance Ivar Bryce invited Fleming to Jamaica to attend a naval conference on Nazi U-boat warfare in the Caribbean as well as to visit his own estate. The serenity of this tropical paradise was a stark contrast to London's war-ravaged urban rubble. No ration books. No food shortages. Spirits that flowed like water. It was too much for an uncompromising, hard-drinking, heavy-smoking aristocrat to resist.

Fleming built Goldeneye, an unpretentious winter escape from London life and his work as a reporter for Kemsley Newspapers Limited. There, he basked in the island's beauty, from January through March, when he wasn't womanizing or gambling.

All of that changed when Fleming found himself waiting at Goldeneye for his pregnant long-time mistress, Lady Anne Rothermere, to finalize her divorce. On February 17, 1952, he sat at his desk and began writing *Casino Royale.*

Drawing heavily on his own life, Fleming described the contents and execution of his perfect "violet hour" libation:

"A dry martini," he said. "One. In a deep champagne goblet."

"Oui, monsieur."

"Just a moment. Three measures of Gordon's, one of vodka, half a measure of Kina Lillet. Shake it very well until it's ice-cold, then add a large thin slice of lemon-peel. Got it?"

Through the guise of James Bond, Fleming justified this recipe by adding:

"I never have more than one drink before dinner. But I do like that one to be large and very strong and very cold and very well-made. I hate small portions of anything, particularly when they taste bad. This drink's my own invention. I'm going to patent it when I can think of a good name."

Though drink historians generally credit the Vesper to Gilberto Preti at London's Dukes Hotel, Preti would have been around fifteen years old when the drink was invented. So who really invented the Vesper?

In his 1975 memoir *You Only Live Once*, Bryce explained how Fleming conjured up the name of the drink and *Casino Royale*'s heroine. While in Jamaica, he came upon the house of an elderly couple and was invited in for evening drinks. Their butler offered him a frozen rum concoction, commenting that "vespers are served." Vespers or evensong is the sixth of the seven canonical hours of the divine office that fall at sunset, the "violet hour."

The drink itself? Bryce and Fleming created the gin-and-vodka cocktail and named it. Fleming inscribed Bryce's presentation copy of *Casino Royale*: "To Ivar, who mixed the first Vesper, and said the good word."

Lillet is a French apéritif wine made by macerating Bordeaux wines with a blend of fruit liqueurs (mostly exotic varieties of orange), and chincona bark (from which quinine is derived). The chincona is the "kina" in the Kina Lillet that James Bond recommended. The name was changed over the years and the formula was modernized a bit (there's less sugar in it now), but it still makes an excellent Martini.

The first drink I invented was **The Thunderer** for *The Times* newspaper. I must have been about twenty-two. It's 50 mls Wyborowa, 2 bar spoons Parfait Amour, 3 drops of crème de cassis stirred and strained into a prechilled Martini glass. Lemon twist. I originally made it with Stoli but *The Times* (via Jane McQuitty, their excellent wine correspondent) didn't like the Russian communist vodka so swapped it for Wyborowa (made by Polmos Polish communists). I make it with Zubrowka now because it tastes better.

—Dick Bradsell

The current roster of California vermouths include Vya, Sutton Cellars, Gallo, Lejon, Gambarelli & Davitto, and Imbue (well, it's Oregon, but still West Coast).

California vermouths that would have been around in Felix Leiter's time include Vai Brothers, Roma, Christian Brothers, Lejon, Santa Alicia, Petri, Lyon's, Chauvel, Italian Swiss Colony, Roman, Franzia, San Martin, Siesta, Grand Monarque, Old Pride, Torino, Mogen David, Parma, Cresta Blanca, Gibson's, and LeFranc,

Felix Leiter—the CIA agent who teamed up with Bond as he battled megalomaniacs like Dr. No and Mr. Big—was no neophyte to fine spirits. He was the embodiment of the debonair American male: cool under fire, loyal to his friends, and a connoisseur of regional cuisine. This Haig & Haig drinker surprised Bond when he ordered a medium-dry Martini with a twist made without the requisite Kina Lillet Blanc.

"Domestic stuff," Leiter explained. "New brand from California. Like it?"

Bond had to admit it was the best vermouth he'd ever tasted.

Our personal adaptation is named **From Russia with Love**, which blends 1 oz. (30 ml) Plymouth gin, 2 oz. (60 ml) Stolichnaya vodka, 0.5 oz. (15 ml) Lillet Blanc, and a dash of Kina bitters. Naturally, it's shaken until it's ice cold and garnished with a lemon twist.

London mixologist extraordinaire Dré Masso created a couple of homages to Fleming's drink in 2006 when the Daniel Craig version of the first Bond novel hit the screen. His **Thyme Vesper** shakes 0.75 oz. (25ml) Wyborowa Exquisite, 1 oz. (30ml) Lillet Blanc, 0.75 oz. (25ml) Beefeater 24 Gin, 1 tsp. sugar syrup, garnished with a fresh thyme sprig and a lemon twist sprayed over the top and then discarded.

Dre's **Red Vesper** shakes 1 oz. (30ml) vodka, 0.5 oz. (15 ml) Lillet Rouge, 0.5 oz. (15 ml) sloe gin, garnished with an orange twist.

A DOSAGE OF VERMOUTH

Vermouth gets its name from the German word for wormwood (*Artemisia absinthium*): **vermut**. A hardy silver-green leafed plant native to Siberia, it's a traditional ingredient found in both absinthe and vermouth. This aromatized wine is macerated with wormwood, juniper berries, coriander, orange peel, cinnamon, cinchona bark, chamomile—as many as forty different botanicals, which have a short life once the bottle is opened, despite fortification with a touch of spirit to retard fermentation. (Never buy a large bottle of vermouth if it's going to sit around for a few months. It quickly loses its character just like any other wine that's had a chance to breathe. Instead, buy a couple smaller ones.)

As an apéritif, vermouth served on the rocks with a citrus twist is a common call in Italian, French, and Spanish cafés. Novelist Ernest Hemingway knew it was manly enough to drink straight and so did the semi-autobiographical hero—Frederic Henry—of his 1929 book **A Farewell to Arms**. While convalescing in an army hospital, Henry offers his night nurse and confidante, Miss Gage, a vermouth. When she returns with the bottle and a glass, he says, "You take the glass. I'll drink from the bottle."

I had never tasted anything so cool and clean. They made me feel civilized.

—Frederic Henry, in reference to his first sip of a Martini, *A Farewell to Arms* (1929)

In deference to those in pursuit of the world's driest Martini, we have included the following photo of Noilly Prat's barrel yard in the south of France. Now, load your mixing glass with ice and gin, and show it this photo—but not for too long.

LUCKY JIM

ADAPTED FROM KINGSLEY AMIS'S RECIPE

Stir

2 oz. (60 ml) Smirnoff vodka

1 tsp. Noilly Prat dry vermouth

1 splash cucumber juice

cucumber slices

Lola's at Century House in Vancouver served a **Joe Average**, made with 2 oz. (60 ml) Stolichnaya vodka and 1 splash Pimm's No. 1, garnished with a cucumber slice and a lemon slice.

Outspoken and irreverent, British novelist Kingsley Amis shared a love of Dry Martinis with his drinking comrades Ian Fleming and John Doxat, preferring a 15:1 formula. Another common bond between Amis and Fleming was James Bond: After Fleming passed away, Amis wrote a Bond adventure in 1968 titled *Colonel Sun*—penned under the nom de guerre Robert Markham—as well as a 1965 character study of the famed superspy, *The James Bond Dossier.*

Amis's first novel, *Lucky Jim,* was a rousing success when it was published in 1954. The protagonist, Jim, wasn't suave or sophisticated. He was a comic anti-hero undergraduate at a provincial university. Amis dedicated a cocktail to his character in his 1970 book *On Drink,* commenting that Jim "would probably make his Clement Freud [*sic*] face if offered one, but he would be among the first to appreciate that its apparent mildness might make it an excellent love-philtre to press on shy young ladies, if there are any of these left anywhere in the land."

The Tatouni shakes 3 oz. (90 ml) Ketel One vodka, 1 splash Martini & Rossi extra-dry vermouth, and 1 splash cucumber juice, garnished with a cucumber slice.

DIRECT MARTINI

ADAPTED FROM A RECIPE BY SALVATORE CALABRESE AT DUKES HOTEL, LONDON

Nestled in a pocket-size cul-de-sac off St. James's Place in London is an intimate shrine to elegant sipping—the bar at Dukes Hotel. Legend has it that long-time regular Ian Fleming was inspired to scribe his line "shaken not stirred" while wiling away a few Martinis in this cocktail sanctuary. We do know that the roster of head bartenders who have presided over guests reads like a Who's Who of London Hotel Mixology—Alessandro Palazzi (2007–present), Gilberto Preti (1983–2004), Salvatore Calabrese (1980–1992).

For years, people said that Gilberto Preti invented the Vesper made famous by Fleming. We now know the truth. Sorry, Gilberto. But you may not know that another Martini was born within these hallowed walls that is neither shaken nor stirred—the Direct Martini—mixed and served from a cocktail trolley that is wheeled tableside so guests can watch the artistry as it happens.

As Salvatore Calabrese explains it, back in 1985, the *San Francisco Chronicle* journalist Stanton Delaplane used to arrive in the bar at midday for a prelunch apéritif. Later in the afternoon, he would return for his usual Martini, commenting, "Salvatore, I want it very, very cold and very dry."

He tried stirring it for longer, then for less time to make it drier. Nothing seemed to make the journalist happy. Then Salvatore came to an epiphany. He poured the vermouth into a bitters bottle to precisely control the dosage—a dash or

No mixing

3 oz. (90 ml) Potocki vodka, frozen for a minimum 24 hours

3 drops extra-dry vermouth

lemon twist

Our own version—**The Seattle**—shakes 2 oz. (60 ml) Russian Standard vodka and 1 dash fresh lemon juice. Take a wet cocktail glass, add a few drops of Angostura bitters, and pop it into the freezer for a few hours. Before straining the drink, mist the prepared glass with extra-dry vermouth from an atomizer to simulate the city's prevailing weather conditions. Then strain and serve.

THE CIVILIZED APPROACH

So how do you hold a Martini glass? A friend said it best: "This depends. One bartender insisted that every Martini had to be as cold as his ex-wife's heart and held 'by the throat.'"

My former employer lifted his Martini with his pinky extended: a strangely dainty gesture for a gentleman built like a heavyweight wrestler. Later, I discovered that he'd broken his pinky and couldn't bend it. (I stopped imitating him.)

One lounge femme fatale seductively suggested that I hold the stem gently between my thumb and forefinger, not high enough to feel the hard chill pulsing through it, but just where I can feel its dampness caress my fingertips.

Unlike a snifter, which has a stubby stem and fits in your hand so that your body heat warms the contents (bringing its subtle flavors to life), a Martini glass is designed to keep your drink cold, but only if you hold it by the stem—not the bowl.

two at most. Then he put the gin bottle and a wet glass in the freezer.

"When Mr. Delaplane came for his usual Martini," Salvatore continued, "I could not wait for him to try my new method. I began by filling the mixing glass with ice. I then took the glass and the bottle from the freezer. When I saw how cold and dry the glass appeared I decided to dispense with the normal method and poured the frozen gin directly into the glass. I then used the bitters bottle to drop the vermouth on top of the gin and obviously added a twist of lemon. In this way the aroma and the flavor of the vermouth plays its part throughout the drinking period. I still remember how, as he tasted it, Mr. Delaplane's eyes, which were always very heavy, began to lift and light up.

"There was no comment! Then he asked for another, tasted it, again no comment! He walked away. At the time I did not know what to think. The next day, he came to the bar and introduced himself as a journalist and showed me a piece that he had written for the *San Francisco Chronicle* which described my Martini as the best that he had ever tried."

The Direct Martini became the keystone of Dukes's cocktail menu: Alessandro and his team make up to two hundred gin or vodka versions of this mixture of precision and showmanship every night. He even conducts private Martini master classes for up to six guests, imparting his knowledge and stories in his remarkably graceful and gracious style.

CLUB MARTINI

ADAPTED FROM PETER DORELLI AT THE AMERICAN BAR AT THE SAVOY, LONDON

There was a time when the American Bar at the Savoy Hotel in London boasted that it was the Martini's birthplace. Admittedly Gin-and-It and Gin-and-French were common calls when Ada Coleman was at the helm, and maybe they were when her predecessor, Fred Meyers, worked the opening night in 1898. One thing's for certain, her successor, Harry Craddock, shook his fair share of Martinis—five different ones. Eddie Clark and Joe Gilmore followed in rapid succession after that. But before the hotel closed for its massive retrofit in 2007, a living legend took the helm, serving his Club Martini to the rich, the famous, and the royal.

During his thirty-five years at the Savoy, Peter Dorelli served the Queen Mother her two parts gin and one part Dubonnet when he opened in the morning. He was even more honored to serve his Club Martini to her in the evening. And before he retired in 2004, Jared got to observe the man in action.

We had spent a long weekend in the Cotswolds, stopping for a few days in London to shop and catch Gilbert & Sullivan's *H.M.S. Pinafore* at the Savoy Theatre. We were dressed more for country than city, but Jared was determined to finally see the American Bar that I had raved about for years. So we went to take a peek, though I doubted we'd get in.

Ahead of us, a midwestern executive couple in matching red and blue tracksuits was being advised by the towering white-jacketed host with a deep, gracious voice that they weren't properly attired

Stir

2 oz. (60 ml) Stolichnaya vodka or Beefeater gin

1 drop Martini & Rossi extra-dry vermouth

a tiny squeeze of lemon oil from the fleshy part of the peel

The sight of all those expensive cars rolling along, crammed to the bulwarks with overfed males and females with fur coats . . . made him feel that he wanted to buy a red tie and a couple of bombs and start the Social Revolution . . . Well, there is, of course, only one thing for a young man to do . . . Mervyn hurried along to the club and in rapid succession drank three Martini cocktails.

—P. G. Wodehouse,
Mulliner Nights

I loved Gilberto Preti at Dukes Hotel bar making Naked Vodka Martinis. We copied it at Dick's Bar at the Atlantic. Hardcore and simple. It's a dash of vermouth in a frozen Martini glass topped with cold Stolichnaya from the freezer.

I prefer very little vermouth and no dilution in my Vodka Martinis.

—Dick Bradsell

and could not get a table in the bar. "Let's go," I whispered to Jared. "We'll come back when we're dressed for the occasion."

They turned to leave, staring at the two of us in our heavy wool sweaters, scarves, and jeans with an all-knowing glare that we were next to be rejected. But the host gave me a wink as Jared spoke up and said, "I know we're not dressed properly. Just wanted to take a peek. We'll come back another time."

"Please," he smiled broadly, "please, come right in. I have an open spot near the bar."

At a cozy table for two, we scanned the menu. A Gin Martini for Jared and a Vodka Martini for me.

Soon the bartender brought two pristine, etched crystal glasses. A classic, 1920s cocktail glass held icy-cold gin and a hint of vermouth. A V-shaped glass of equal height bearing vodka was positioned before me. We sipped in silence, knowing that we had to leave in fifteen minutes to catch the overture next door.

Jared flagged down the waiter and said, "This is the best Martini I've ever tasted. Is Mr. Dorelli making them? Please pass on my compliments."

We finished our drinks and looked for the waiter, ready to dash across to the theater. He was standing over a group of expensively suited gentlemen a couple of tables away, and asked them to leave saying they were too loud. "Sorry, Mr. Dorelli," one replied with a laugh as he took the bill. "We'll try to be better tomorrow."

As Jared made the connection, Mr. Dorelli disappeared, then arrived a minute later at our table, replacing our empty glasses with another round.

What could we do? We missed the opening song, "Buttercup," but we didn't care. How could you refuse a second round of the best Martini ever?

Years later, Peter finally admitted he'd recognized me instantly from my years of visits, but would never risk embarrassing a lady who arrived in his bar with a man he didn't know by greeting her by name.

In another submission to our 1996 Shaken Not Stirred Martini Story Competition, Ernesto Paez, an Argentine living in Copenhagen, devised a potent concoction called **The Argentine-Arctic Kick**, blending 3 oz. (90 ml) freezer-chilled vodka (a 50-50 blend of Finlandia and Stolichnaya), garnished with 2 stuffed green olives that were marinated in Martini & Rossi extra-dry vermouth.

We recently ticked another box on our bucket list of things to do in this lifetime. We not only spent a night at the Savoy Hotel, but on arrival we were greeted by all the fixings to mix a round (a few rounds really) of Martinis: a bottle of Sipsmith gin, Martini dry vermouth, orange bitters in a silver-topped dasher, a crystal mixing glass, silver mixing spoon and strainer, an Amalfi lemon, house marinated olives, and ice. While Erik Lorincz has ensured the bar is every bit as good as when Harry Craddock mixed the drinks, it was a personal pleasure to stir our own while enjoying the London panorama.

NAIRN FALLS

CREATED BY JARED BROWN AND ANISTATIA MILLER

Let stand without ice
2 oz. (60 ml) Beluga vodka
0.5 oz. (15 ml) Retsina Blanc

lemon twist or lemon-cured olive

This particular recipe requires no ice. An icy, rushing body of water-a babbling brook, a white-water river, a glacial stream or lake-will do just fine. (However, we don't advise trying this at the ocean.)

For those of you who've never tasted retsina, this bone-dry Greek wine is aged in pine casks, so it takes on the flavor of the great outdoors.

Ah, camping season! The time when real men, women—and even lowly house pets—forsake the comforts of civilization (Martinis excepted, of course), and head for the untrammeled depths of the wilderness. Happy campers that we are, we assembled only the barest essentials: tent; air mattress; flannel sheet; duvet; pillows; three-burner propane stove; stainless steel pots and pans; enamel dinnerware; cutlery; glassware; a well-stocked, black leather, vintage port-a-bar; mobile phone; laptop; camera; binoculars; sunscreen; bug repellent; citronella candles; flashlights; and gold-sifting pans. We popped over to the local Hertz office, rented a Ford Explorer, and set out to get close to nature in the alpine beauty of Nairn Falls just above Whistler, British Columbia. We forgot one thing—vermouth. Oh well, retsina made a reasonable substitute.

So how do you chill a Martini on the second day when all the ice in the cooler has melted? Mountain glaciers around us beckoned. All that ice—but alas, just out of reach. We remembered something W. C. Fields said, "Once . . . in the wilds of Afghanistan, I lost my corkscrew, and we were forced to live on nothing but food and water for days."

We dove into the rushing Green River to cool off. It was a nice hot day, but somehow, if that water hadn't been moving so fast, it would've frozen solid. A shock wave of inspiration transpired. We duct-taped the lid onto a full shaker, wrapped a twenty-pound fishing line around it, and affixed it with more duct tape.

Then we cast it out into the milky green water, *et voilà*! Shaken and chilled!

But we do have a word of recent experience: Never attempt to duct-tape a wet shaker (with apologies to those drunken fish). One fishing tale is never enough, so here's one that CBC broadcaster Coreen Larson told us:

It was another blazing hot summer day on the Canadian Prairies. Some friends and I decided that the only way to cool off was to try our hand, line, and luck at fishing. The prospect of spending four and a half hours floating around a calm and beautiful lake with a boatful of notorious beer drinkers was bittersweet. The moment reeked of a Dry Martini and I knew it, but what could I do in the wilderness? I had to think fast.

Luckily, I came prepared. In an old tin lunch box, I packed a tiny little mickey of Tanqueray (I knew that mickeys were good for more than just drunken nights at high school dances), a jar full of vermouth (don't tell Noilly Prat), six green olives in a mini-Mason jar, a travel-size cocktail shaker, and a bucket full of ice on the side. All this with the essence of Dean Martin and we were "gone fishin'" . . . woo wee!

Just when I thought it couldn't get any better—me with a full Martini, my Len Thompson hook dangling in the water and the sound of roaring motor boats and jet-skis singing quietly in the background—something happened that was orgasmic in proportion. I felt a tug on my line (if you know what I mean) and felt what had to be the biggest fish in the world trying to ingest my Len Thompson! I had to make a choice, and for the first time in my life, I gave up my Martini to reel in my catch. I handed it faithfully over to my fishing partner, Bartley Melnechenko, and

On November 22, 1995, quiz competitors (a group of University of Manitoba and Carleton University professors) on an episode of the Discovery Channel's *Discovery Connection* were given a bonus question:

According to scientists, shaking a Vodka Martini . . .

1. does nothing to alter the drink.

2. excites the alcohol molecules to jump down your throat.

3. increases the alcohol concentration.

4. causes tiny bubbles to make the taste less oily.

5. oxidizes molecules called aldehydes to make the taste sharper.

The answer: choices 4 and 5.

had him hold my glass to my lips as I frantically tried to reel in the first fresh water shark in Saskatchewan! Though my heart pounded and my physical and emotional strength faded, I felt tranquillity with every new sip of Martini. It was pure ecstasy.

Time stood still as I pulled in that weighty load. At times I felt like I was making no progress with the aquatic beast, but the gin restored my confidence. I'll never forget that moment on Child's Lake that August afternoon. The sun, the friends, the Dry Martini with two olives—shaken not stirred—and the "one that got away."

Even if you're stuck in the city, surrounded by nothing more exotic than pigeons, poodles, and the occasional potted plant, the Nairn Falls is sure to answer the call of the wild.

In another submission to our 1996 Shaken Not Stirred Martini Story Competition, Dave Kaspryzk's fishy variation, the **Mariner's Martini**, is guaranteed to trim your sails: Substitute a whole anchovy or an anchovy-stuffed olive for the Nairn Falls garnish.

The **Octopus Martini** that was served at Ken Stewart's Grille in Akron, Ohio, used a smoked baby octopus and a lemon twist as a garnish. A variation on that theme, the **Octopus's Garden Martini**, replaces the twist with a black olive.

OLIVER'S CLASSIC MARTINI

CREATED AT OLIVER'S AT THE MAYFLOWER PARK HOTEL

When we first put up our Web site, on Halloween night 1995, one visitor wrote to us, asking about the Seattle Martini Competition. We'd never heard of it and put out an all-points bulletin for more information. After a few months, we finally tracked down the event's founder, Marc Nowak, who explained why he started it:

In 1991, there was this place down the street named Von's Roasthouse that had a giant banner on it saying: "Best Martinis in Town." Our customers would walk in and say: "Their Martinis are terrible, yours are much better." Anyway, we challenged them, but they wouldn't play! (Guess they didn't want to lose their banner.) So we challenged them in the press. They still wouldn't play.

By this time, we decided to make it an open challenge. Boy, we got takers. The Four Seasons was in there in about two seconds; the Met Grill was another first challenger. Plus, we had a bunch of other restaurants. We narrowed it down by reputation and taste tests, figuring we could manage five, which [with two Martinis at each place] was a mistake, and ended up cutting it down to four bars the year afterward. It's just grown from there. The first time [in 1992], we had sixty people, now there are hundreds. And it's turned into a very black-tie affair. It's a riot!

Oliver's at the Mayflower Park Hotel was the perennial winner for Best Classic Martini at the Seattle Martini Competition, save for one time. After tasting it for ourselves, we know why.

Shake

2.5 oz. (75 ml) Skyy vodka

0.25 oz. (10 ml) Cinzano dry vermouth

2 vermouth-marinated green olives

Pour the vermouth into a mixing glass. Swirl to coat, then drain. Fill the prepared glass with ice. Add the vodka and shake vigorously. Let stand for about 20 seconds. Place the olives on the edge of a chilled cocktail glass and strain the drink over the olives.

Gin aficionados shouldn't despair, Oliver's also makes this classic recipe with Bombay Sapphire Gin.

MOLOTOV COCKTAIL

CREATED BY LOREN DUNSWORTH AT LOLA'S AT CENTURY HOUSE, VANCOUVER

Shake

3 oz. (90 ml) Stolichnaya vodka

0.5 oz. (15 ml) Jameson Irish Whiskey

0.5 oz. (15 ml) Irish Mist liqueur

In all our research we've encountered plenty of drinks that are ignited before they're served, but we never came across a single flaming Martini. There are two good reasons. First, and most obvious: fire is hot, Martinis should be cold. And second, you generally make a Martini out of the best ingredients you can afford; surely there's something of less value that you can set on fire.

Not to be confused with the gasoline bottle garnished with a bit of rag, this Molotov Cocktail is a far more sociable beverage, capable of igniting lively conversation with a hint of the blarney. However, born pyromaniacs do need a little more satisfaction from their Martinis than the subtle smoky hint found in Irish whiskey. Steve Starr has a flamboyant option for their consideration:

This was first demonstrated to me by a bartender named Kimon at the Lion Bar in Chicago. I was there fifteen years ago and ordered a Martini with a lemon twist. Kimon asked me if I wanted it "smoked." It was a little noisy and I couldn't understand what he was saying, so I just said yes.

You make a regular Martini (preferably, in my opinion, with gin and straight up) in a classic glass. It must be ordered with a lemon peel garnish. Now, before you drop the lemon peel into the Martini, light a match, warm the peel with it, then crisply squeeze the peel over the flame. If done correctly, there will be a brief but spectacular "poof" of light and a little smoke. Immediately drop the lemon peel into the Martini. This adds a very subtle but distinctive smoky texture to the drink.

In essence, the Smoked Martini is half show and half taste. The lemon peel should have just a touch of the inner lemon (not just the rind) attached to it. The real tricky part is to be able to do the Smoked Martini by yourself.

Holding the match and the lemon peel in just the right way allows you to squeeze the lemon peel and at the same time bring the lit match right in front of the yellow side of the peel as it twists, resulting in the flameout. At first, though, it's probably necessary to have a friend help by holding the match while you twist the peel or vice versa, just so you can see what the effect should be.

Here's how this works. Lemon oil—which is trapped in the pores of the lemon rind—is highly flammable. (No, this doesn't mean that your lemons are likely to spontaneously combust and blow the door off the refrigerator.) When you squeeze a twist, it sprays little bits of oil out. Don't point the twist toward your eyes, even without a lit match, because the oil stings. Each twist is good for only one spray. After that, any oil that was destined to fly has already done so (although flaming the second squeeze is a safe way to practice your technique). This works only with fresh lemons. That shrunken yellow thing in the bottom of the fridge has already lost its oil—and flavor—to dehydration.

I first saw a twist flamed at the famous Mamma Leone's Restaurant in the early 1970s. The old Italian waiters flamed a lemon peel into the espresso at the end of the meal . . . JUST at tip time and probably had been for 50 years!

Then the next time I encountered it was at Chasen's Restaurant in Beverly Hills, CA, where Pepe Ruiz used it to garnish Dean Martin's Flame of Love Martini.

I wanted the Cosmopolitans at Rainbow Room to be special so I used the Cointreau, fresh lime, and added the flaming orange peel.

—Dale DeGroff

(See page 186 for more information about the Flame of Love and page 146 for the Cosmopolitan story.)

Audrey Saunders made a **Dreamy Dorini Smoking Martini** for her friend Dori Bryant, shaking 0.5 oz. (15 ml) Laphroaig 10-Year Scotch, 2 oz. (60 ml) Absolut vodka, and 5 drops Pernod.

To make a **Smoked Martini**, make your favorite classic, but before you garnish the drink with a lemon twist, hold the peel over the drink, squeeze the twist, and simultaneously light it with a match. When it finishes its flameout, drop the twist into the drink. For a complete Siegfried and Roy presentation, use an oversize twist and play Arthur Brown Jr.'s 1960s hit song, "Fire."

THE BOTTOM LINE ON VODKA MARTINIS

The hijacking of the name Martini for the Vodka Martini (soon to become just straight up vodka), is the great unreported crime of the twentieth century.

To take the name of the most celebrated example of what a balanced cocktail is, and attach it to a drink that is the very opposite of balance, is truly a sin.

Never mind the blatant disrespect to one's father's generation, or the lack of confidence shown by being unwilling to try to create a name of one's own. It is the sheer scope of the ignorance of intentionally replacing something well-balanced with a blunt instrument that leaves me without words.

It's as if the Sex Pistols had hedged their bets by calling themselves Louis Armstrong and His Hot Fives, and no one noticed.

—Sasha Petraske

By now you may have a better understanding of how vodka rushed up on American and British shores to overtake gin in Martinis. It does help when you've got an entire government using its marketing muscle to export its monopolized product. It certainly doesn't hurt to have a savvy marketing mind behind a product with provenance. That happened twice in vodka history: once with Heublein's John Martin getting behind Smirnoff and once more when Michael Roux took the century-old Swedish vodka Absolut and made it a household word.

But marketing wasn't the only reason vodka laid siege and won the battle in bars. You see, during the 1930s, the United States, China, and most of Europe experienced grain shortages because of droughts and bad farming practices. Britain's harvests also fell short of expectations. Government hoarding of grain for the forthcoming war effort cut off supplies for spirits production. This forced gin producers to use nongrain spirit for production throughout the war years. Then postwar grain rationing left them no option but to continue rectifying gin with sugar-based spirit. The British Royal Navy even canceled its 145-year standing order for Plymouth Gin, because it wasn't up to snuff. (Plymouth announced that the grain was back in a 1961 ad campaign to the great relief of gin drinkers everywhere.)

Why did the vermouth disappear from this alternative to the classic Silver Bullet? Because the Vichy government of Nazi-occupied France banned, in 1940, the production, sale, and consumption of vermouth, except for production that was intended for export. Other apéritifs with an alcohol by volume content of less than 16 percent were permitted for consumption four days a week. Vermouth did not qualify. No wonder the legend persisted that Winston Churchill took the French vermouth in hand and bowed toward France rather than put it in his Martini! He didn't know when he was going to get another bottle!

In defense of vodka and Vodka Martinis, Anistatia has one more comment:

> I have been a vodka "snob" for more than four decades. In just the same way that I walk into a bar and dictate what brands of gin and vermouth go into my 3:1 Dry Martini and my 1:1 Martini with Italian vermouth, I dictate what vodka I want chilled to the bone and served in a cocktail glass. Those dictates are based on dozens of tasting sessions to educate my palate.
>
> Based on my "lady's whim," I have a specific brand attached to potato vodka, rye vodka, barley vodka, wheat vodka. Each offers a different character: green pepper, black pepper, marshmallow, soft vanilla. The ones I mix with are not the same ones that I drink as shots or as Vodka Martinis.
>
> It drives me mental when people slough me off as a slave to marketing rather than understanding that I treat every spirit category in the same manner. (You should see me when we're in Scotland surrounded by all those gorgeous whiskeys. No one calls me a slave to that!)

The subjectivity that surrounds the Martini goes even further than debates on execution and proportion; historical events added the selection of spirit to the mix and contributed to its evolution.

I think we just made an important medical discovery. If you act drunk long enough, you can get a hangover.

—Hawkeye Pierce,
M*A*S*H

SIPPING SIBLINGS
VERMOUTH FAMILY CLASSICS

The Martini shares its glass with a menu of other cocktails pairing spirit with vermouth, and we'd like to dive into a few of them. Complex and sophisticated. Elegant, yet open to variation. Classics built on quality rather than the number of their ingredients. That's the simplest description we can offer of the vermouth family. We became entranced by this extended family while we were writing *The Mixellany Guide to Vermouth & Other Aperitifs.* When vermouth made its way from cafés as a straight pour or main ingredient (yes, there once was a Vermouth Cocktail) to saloons and cocktail bars in a supporting role to each of the major spirits categories, it evoked poetry, debate, literary and poetic wax, and manic subjectivity on its use.

There has never been a debate as to what vermouth brings to the table: roundness and richness of flavor, accentuation of good spirits, a symphony of subtle bitter and sweet botanical notes. There is a reason vermouth has been such an enduring cocktail ingredient. It is a perfect mixer and modifier for spirits. There is also a reason it fell out of favor and is now returning rapidly: It takes a bit of skill and understanding to mix with vermouth.

Need another reason to savor vermouth-based cocktails at a time when it seems like every bartender is in love with their citrus squeezer and desperate to foist another icy goblet of fruit acid on you every time you ask them what's new? The citrus in a Daiquirí is enough to temporarily soften the enamel on your teeth. Brush immediately after and you're stripping enamel. And pity the barman who diligently straw-tastes each of them. No wonder they're all using sensitive-teeth toothpaste these days. The antidote? Have cheese with those margaritas or, better yet, stick to drinks with a vermouth base instead.

A few tips before we delve into the origins and the myriad modern variations on these classic recipes. Think of these as the six commandments for incorporating vermouth into your drinks repertoire.

1. Vermouth should always be used fresh. (Have we already said this? Good! It bears repeating.) The botanicals and wine, while stabilized from further fermentation, do lose subtlety and complexity with oxidation over time.

2. Always refrigerate vermouth (or at least store it in a cool, dark place) after opening to retard oxidation. It is a wine. It may be fortified and stouter of constitution than a beaujolais, but it is still a wine. It has less alcohol on average than port.

3. After months in the refrigerator, vermouth is still good for cooking but less so for drinking.

4. Vermouth is excellent for reducing the ABV of mixed drinks, for more responsible service, without detracting from a cocktail's strength of flavor.

5. Shaking a drink with vermouth causes it to cloud and foam slightly, while it intensifies the flavor. If you want clarity in a Martini or Manhattan you should stir the drink. However, shaking will not damage the flavor, so there is nothing wrong with shaking a drink that contains vermouth.

6. An excellent solution for keeping fresh vermouth on hand is to buy 375 ml bottles. Minis, kept chilled in the vegetable crisper of your refrigerator, are even better. Unopened, and kept away from sun and intense heat, a bottle of vermouth will keep for years.

You now know how well vermouth works with gin and vodka. Let's start with the Martini's kissing cousin, the Manhattan.

MANHATTAN COCKTAIL

INVENTED AT THE MANHATTAN CLUB, NEW YORK

The Manhattan Cocktail may or may not have been born at the Manhattan Club when it was at Fifth Avenue and Thirty-fourth Street in New York City, but there is no doubt it was popularized there (though not, as legend would have it, by Manhattan socialite Jennie Jerome—she was at Blenheim Palace in the United Kingdom for her son Winston Churchill's birth and christening at the time she supposedly invented it). When the club published a fiftieth anniversary book for its members in 1915, it included its secret recipe and staked its claim that they had given birth to the world's most popular whiskey drink, in 1865, when the club opened.

Harry "the Dean" Johnson added a couple of flourishes to his 1888 version, including a dash of gomme syrup and a dash of curaçao or absinthe, garnished with a lemon twist.

In a mere thirty years the recipe got a little sweeter and spicier with the introduction of Angostura bitters as a replacement for orange bitters. One of the most famous bartenders of that era was Willie "the Only William" Schmidt, whose bar once stood on the spot that is now more or less precisely the center point of Ground Zero at the World Trade Center in New York. His 1891 recipe demonstrated this shift in public preference.

Stir

1 oz. (30 ml) bourbon or rye whiskey

1 oz. (30 ml) Italian vermouth

2 dashes orange bitters

orange twist or a Luxardo cherry

"I wanted to make a vodka-based cocktail that had the complexity and character of a Manhattan," Dré Masso said when he created the **New Amsterdam Cocktail**, shaking 1 oz. (30 ml) Wyborowa Exquisite, 1 oz. (30 ml) Dubonnet Rouge, 1 oz. (30 ml) Kahlúa, and 2 dashes Angostura bitters, garnished with an orange twist.

In the 1860s, cocktails were regarded as morning drinks, served to relieve such ailments as "whiskey in the hair" or "hot coppers."

ROB ROY COCKTAIL

Stir

1 oz. (30 ml) blended Scotch whiskey

1 oz. (30 ml) Italian vermouth

2 dashes Angostura bitters

Blended Scotch whiskey made the headlines during the 1890s more than once. Industrial magnate Andrew Carnegie, the "Laird of Cluny Castle," made quite a stir, in 1890, when he ordered a barrel of scotch whiskey to be imported and delivered to U.S. president Benjamin Harrison at the White House.

The world's first motion picture commercial was produced and displayed, in 1897, high above Herald Square in Manhattan. The subject? DEWAR'S SCOTCH WHISKY. (It consisted of a couple of apparently drunk guys in kilts dancing around a small table with a whiskey bottle on it; the cameraman likely helped them drink it, as he managed to get only part of the awning into the ad so it read "war's Whisky" in the background.)

In December 1894, music critic and comic opera composer Reginald De Koven premiered his operetta *Rob Roy* on Broadway. Similar in style to Gilbert and Sullivan, De Koven's work often spun off into hit songs of the day. Such was the case with Rob Roy's "Dearest of My Heart" and "My Home Is Where the Heather Blooms." His operetta obviously struck a chord in Manhattan because a namesake drink appeared on cocktail menus up and down Broadway—the Rob Roy Cocktail.

Hugo R. Ensslin, chronicler of the Aviation, provided a "perfect" version of the Rob Roy a decade later while working at the Hotel Wallick in Manhattan. Called the Affinity, it adds a touch more spice and dryness.

Another drink that owes its name to the overwhelming success of a play, a song, or a book is the Trilby. Written by George du Maurier and serialized in Harper's in 1894, *Trilby* tells the story of a tone-deaf girl who works as an artist's model and laundress in Paris who is transformed by the hypnotist Svengali into an operatic diva. A triangle forms when a young artist also falls in love with her. The novel struck a chord that sang for decades. Its popularity ran second only to Bram Stoker's 1897 novel *Dracula*.

Trilby inspired Gaston Leroux to write the 1910 novel *The Phantom of the Opera*, which also spun over into an equally successful play that was revived numerous times into the 1920s. (The Trilby hat was an indirect spinoff of the play, in which one of the characters sported this narrow style of brim.)

Obviously, de Maurier's novel also chimed in Harry Johnson's ear. He published a recipe for the Trilby Cocktail in the 1900 edition of his *Bartenders' Manual*.

Hugo R. Ensslin's **Affinity Cocktail** stirred 1 oz. (30 ml) blended Scotch whiskey with 0.5 oz. (15 ml) Italian vermouth, 0.5 oz. (15 ml) French vermouth, and 2 dashes Angostura bitters, garnished with a lemon twist.

Harry Johnson's **Trilby Cocktail** stirred 1 oz. (30 ml) blended Scotch whiskey with 1 oz. (30 ml) Italian vermouth, 2 dashes absinthe, 2 dashes orange bitters, 2 dashes Parfait d'Amour, garnished with maraschino cherries and a lemon twist.

Violet-hued Parfait d'Amour disappeared from the **Trilby Cocktail** in the 1935 Old Mr. Boston Official Bartender's Guide, which shook 1 oz. (30 ml) blended Scotch whiskey with 0.5 oz. (15 ml) Italian vermouth, and 2 dashes orange bitters.

Harry Craddock tipped his hat to Rudolph Valentino's 1922 box office hit with the **Blood & Sand Cocktail**, shaking 1 oz. (30 ml) blended Scotch whiskey with 0.75 oz. (20 ml) Italian vermouth, 1 oz. (30 ml) sanguinello juice (aka: blood orange juice), and 0.75 (20 ml) Cherry Heering.

EL PRESIDENTE COCKTAIL

POPULARIZED BY EDDIE WOELKE AT SEVILLA-BILTMORE HOTEL, HAVANA

Shake

1 oz. (30 ml) Havana Club Añejo
3 Años Rum

1 oz. (30 ml) French vermouth

1 dash grenadine or curaçao

orange twist

A judge and a congressman were having lunch in a Miami café. The politician was on his second double El Presidente, and despite his cajoling, the judge was still sipping an iced tea. "Say, have you ever tried a Presidente?" the politician asked. "No," the judge replied, "but I've tried a few people who did."

You could call it the Rum Martini or Manhattan. El Presidente, when it is mixed properly, stands proudly alongside both—a sophisticated drink more suited to a jacket-required Havana nightclub than a sandy beachside bar. This is the sort of drink that pairs well with a good cigar and holds its own before a steak (or roast suckling pig).

In 1928, British playwright and journalist Basil Woon published a drinking man's portrait of Prohibition-era Havana, *When It's Cocktail Time in Cuba*. In this meaty volume, he detailed his encounters in the island country's casinos, country clubs, and, naturally, its cocktail bars.

He cited the Daiquiri as the most popular refreshment of the "earnest drinkers of Havana." Yet despite his detailed account of its compounding, Woon proclaimed another drink "the aristocrat of cocktails" and deemed it "the one preferred by the better class of Cubans." That drink is El Presidente.

Where was it born? "The Sevilla-Biltmore is to Havana what the Ritz is to Paris, headquarters of the wealthy pleasure seeker," Woon wrote. Twice daily, the Old-Timers' Club—an informal gathering of prominent expats and businessmen—gathered to share the creations of Eddie Woelke and Fred Kaufman.

Across the hotel's long mahogany bar, Kaufman mixed a variety of original creations that featured pineapple juice. His most notable concoction, of course, was the Mary Pickford, which is frequently miscredited to Woelke or even Constante

Ribaligua Vert at El Floridita. However, Eddie Woelke was famed for Mint Juleps that Woon swore would cause "any Southern gentleman to yelp the rebel yell."

Born in Philadelphia in 1877, Eddie worked his way up to some of the world's finest watering holes. From the Germantown Cricket Club in his hometown he made his way to the Plaza Athenée in Paris, where he met his wife. Returning to the United States, he presided in 1906 at New York's Knickerbocker Hotel with a young Harry Craddock at his side and then at the New York Biltmore when it opened seven years later. With a stroke of great luck he was invited, in 1919, by its owners to be part of the opening team at their new property, Havana's Sevilla-Biltmore Hotel on Calle Trocadero.

General Mario García Menocal y Deop had been Cuba's president since his election on May 20, 1913. He was still in office when the hotel welcomed dignitaries, celebrities, and masters of industry to visit this crown jewel of hospitality.

Is it possible that Eddie put this drink on the menu to honor a visit from El Presidente? We may never know for sure. But popular lore claims this was the politician's favorite quaff before he was voted out of office two years later. Eddie moved on to the Casino Nacional in 1924 (and some people say he also did a stint at the Havana-American Jockey Club) when the Sevilla-Biltmore was closed for renovation. Who knows if he was responsible? But when President Gerardo Machado was voted into office the following year, El Presidente was slightly modified and renamed Presidente Machado.

A note on rum: Cuban rum has more in common with rhum agricole than with rum. So, if you live in a country where it's against the law to line Castro's pockets, try an agricole.

Our good friend London master mixologist Nick Strangeway modernized his version of this Cuban classic, giving the drink a deep character. **Strangeway's El Presidente** shakes 1.5 oz. (45 ml) Havana Club Añejo Especial, 0.75 oz. (20 ml) Lillet Blanc, and 1 splash curaçao, garnished with an orange twist and a cocktail cherry.

Woelke's **Presidente Machado** shakes 1 oz. (30 ml) Havana Club Añejo Blanco, 1 oz. (30 ml) French vermouth, 1 dash grenadine, and 1 dash curaçao, garnished with an orange twist.

During Prohibition, at Sloppy Joe's in Old Havana, they didn't mind being called a "speakout-loud" and went so far as to dress their doorman as a policeman to greet American tourists and welcome them into the bar.

El Presidente's and Presidente Machado's popularity continued in Havana's bars even after the Cuban president was exiled in 1933. Charles H. Baker discovered it at El Floridita later in the decade. Constante Ribaligua Vert preferred to have his staff garnish it with a cocktail cherry. The Cuban bartenders' guild took a slight step back to Woelke's recipe and a baby step forward when they standardized the recipe in their 1945 edition of *El Arte del Cantinero*.

We know that Machado was proud enough of his version to present it to another dignitary: Calvin Coolidge, who was U.S. president during the height of Prohibition. An item appeared in the January 17, 1928, edition of *The Evening Independent* that noted that "although the state dinner given by President Machado of Cuba at the presidential palace last night in honor of President Coolidge was exceedingly wet, starting with a fiery 'presidente cocktail' and ending with fine old 1811 brandy, guests at the dinner insisted that President Coolidge did not drink any of the wines or liquors."

Or did he? American newspapermen at the scene tried to pry details from guests and officials but none were forthcoming, so they declared without witnessing the dinner that Coolidge had scrupulously abstained.

The Cuban bartenders guild standardized **El Presidente Cocktail** in 1945, shaking 1 oz. (30 ml) Cuban silver rum, 1 oz. (30 ml) French vermouth, and 1 dash grenadine, garnished with an orange twist and a cocktail cherry.

The **Perfect Presidente** served at Victor's Café in Miami shakes 1.5 oz. (45 ml) Bacardi Superior rum, 0.75 oz. (25 ml) Italian vermouth, 0.5 oz. (15 ml) French vermouth, and 1 teaspoon grenadine, garnished with a cocktail cherry.

SOMBRERO COCKTAIL

DOCUMENTED BY WILLIAM J. TARLING, LONDON

You might be surprised to see tequila in this family. Yet the quintessential Mexican distillate met vermouth ages ago, in the most unlikely of places—London. It happened while the Bright Young People frolicked into the wee hours in and around Piccadilly Circus at the Café Royal, Ciro's Club, and the Criterion.

Before the curtain drew on the devil-may-care era spanning from 1920 to 1939, the British bartending profession showed its might and muscle, forming the United Kingdom Bartenders' Guild, the first of its kind.

And then one of its presidents, William J. Tarling, published a compendium of what London barmen were serving in the 1937 *Café Royal Cocktail Book*. One of the first cocktail books to offer up tequila-based drinks, its Matador and Sombrero joined the vermouth family.

Shake

0.75 oz. (20 ml) silver tequila

0.75 oz. (20 ml) Italian vermouth

0.75 oz. (20 ml) French vermouth

squeeze a lemon twist over the top

John Wayne was a big fan of tequila, which he dubbed "Mexican whiskey." It has been called pulque, mezcal wine, cactus juice, and many other misleading names. It is a distillate of the Blue Weber Tequiliana agave plant, a desert succulent. It is made by roasting the piña, the heart of the plant, then grinding it, fermenting and distilling it. Always look for "100% agave" on the label.

William Tarling's **Matador Cocktail** shakes 1 oz. (30 ml) silver tequila, 0.5 oz. (15 ml) French vermouth, and 0.5 oz. (15 ml) Italian vermouth, garnished with a squeeze of lemon twist on top.

METROPOLE COCKTAIL

DOCUMENTED BY ALBERT STEVENS CROCKETT, NEW YORK

Stir

1 oz. (30 ml) cognac

1 oz. (30 ml) French vermouth

1 dash Peychaud's bitters

1 dash orange bitters

cocktail cherry

On the way to Newark Airport, a limo driver asked us what we do for a living. "How do you survive? I get terrible hangovers!" We explained our secret—a glass of water for every drink during the evening. He stared at us in the rearview mirror for an unnervingly long moment (remember, he was driving). Then he said, "How the heck am I supposed to get through sixteen large glasses of water in one evening?!"

The oaky dimensions of cognac work well with the bittersweet aspects of vermouth, and so foreign news correspondent Albert Stevens Crockett believed when he wrote his 1931 book *Old Waldorf Bar Days*. Prohibition in the United States was on its last legs and Crockett's book paid misty-eyed homage to the cocktail's golden age, reminding readers of the joys of social sipping in the world's finest establishments. A drink that he "attributed to a once well-known and somewhat lively hotel, whose bar was long a center of life after dark in the Times Square district" was the Metropole.

Crockett also documented the **Adonis Cocktail**, named after Edward Everett Rice's 1894 Broadway hit, stirring 1 oz. (30 ml) sherry, 1 oz. (30 ml) Italian vermouth, and 2 dashes orange bitters.

THE BOTTOM LINE
ON THE SIPPING SIBLINGS

The Martini evolved from the original Cock-tail. Before the Martini there was the Gin Cocktail. And when vermouth arrived in the United States, the Vermouth Cock-tail was born. Both cocktails are slightly imbalanced. The Gin Cocktail is strong, but could use a bit more complexity. The Vermouth Cocktail nearly makes up for its softness with a spectrum of flavors that range far off the charts. With the Martini, the two elements came together.

There are reports from the 1870s of people taking their Vermouth Cocktails with a bit of brandy. The inevitable leaps occurred with vermouth being fortified with whiskey in the hands of people such as Willy "the Baron" Schmidt, New York's most publicized 1890s mixologist. Go anywhere in the world and you'd find vermouth mingling with another spirit: rum in Havana, tequila in London, vodka in New York, amaros in Milan.

Vermouth made the three-element cocktail equation into a work of mathematical and gustatory perfection. When the vermouth dried up during the Second World War, the equation was the only vestige left, along with a bunch of liquor in search of a mate.

The world searched for ways to make the iconic stemmed cocktail glass work with that same level of complexity and visual beauty that the Martini and her sipping siblings offered. That is our next pit stop on this spirituous journey.

Politicians stepped in during Prohibition to alleviate one of the most egregious hangovers (long before The Hangover *was filmed). It began in California, where a young bachelor assemblyman championed a 1927 bill "banning gin marriages." To prevent people from going out for a night of drinking and then waking up married, he instituted a three-day waiting period between applying for and receiving a marriage license. Other states followed suit.*

CHAPTER TWO
SPECIALS
The Modern Martini Renaissance

We've been in trouble ever since we first wrote *Shaken Not Stirred®: A Celebration of the Martini,* in 1996, because we talked about cocktails that get served in cocktail glasses and were dubbed Martinis. We weren't the only ones who opted to mix dozens of short drinks, serve them straight up in stemmed glasses, and call them Martinis.

We did it because we felt the Martini conveyed the message that the drink we were discussing was going to be small, icy cold, and—let's admit it—look downright sexy. No soda. No ginger ale. Just a drink with passion. A see-through with style. That's why we call them Modern Martinis.

This drink category had its birth when a new generation discovered romance and indulgence were still possible, even as the early 1980s recession cut the cash flow, limiting most people's ability to afford luxuries. The hippy decades of sex and drugs and rock 'n' roll were over. A 1950s revival sparked the return of neon, diners, and movies like *Back to the Future.* With it came the search for a little of the '50s sophistication, a little of their self-indulgence. People once again settled into cocktail-hour consciousness just like 1950s working stiffs who stopped off for a Martini or three on the way home.

Somehow any cocktail just tastes more grown up in the V-shaped glass and that lengthy stem.

—Loren Dunsworth,
Lola's Restaurant,
West Hollywood

The Martini is probably the most recognized cocktail in the world. There have been several generations of the Martini. It continues to evolve and change. Now not one singular cocktail, but a huge category of its own, there is a style of Martini for everyone. Respect!

—Dré Masso

In her 1991 book *The Popcorn Report*, trend guru Faith Popcorn predicted that a resurgence of the "Cocktail Hour at Home" would become a facet of "Socialized Cocooning." People began to invite close friends over or head to a home-away-from-home bar rather than huddling alone at home or hitting big anonymous establishments. During the 1990s recession a tribal mentality blossomed. Making Cosmos at home while your own live version of *Friends* watched *Sex and the City* or *24* was a weekly ritual along with checking out the newest classic cocktail "speakeasy."

Popcorn predicted, in 2007, that "Pleasure Revenge" (read: a desire for selective indulgence despite the recession) and "Cashing Out" (read: rejecting hyper-consumption because it's excessive and physically damaging to humans and to the planet) would drive consumer purchases in the 2010s.

What does that mean for Martini lovers? Making cocktails at home for yourself and friends lets you celebrate without breaking the budget or the driving laws. The savings also means that you and your gang get hands-on mixing opportunities and can splurge on occasional nights of "research" at high-end cocktail bars for inspiration.

Let's face it. Binge drinking isn't fun, it's for amateurs and people who really shouldn't drink. A cocktail made with premium spirits and fresh ingredients can satiate even the strongest hankering for intensity. Umami: It is possible to achieve that satisfying savory balance we all desire. Join us down this exciting new garden path.

WARNING

We interrupt this book, taking a page out of the 1952 revised edition of **The Savoy Cocktail Book**, which contained endpaper warnings about certain drinks that appeared in the original edition. Following is a list of Modern Martinis (as well as some old woofers) that appeared in the first edition of **Shaken Not Stirred®: A Celebration of the Martini** and do not appear in this version. May they rest in peace like long wallet chains and suspenders on Levi's.

Alexander Nevsky Martini
American Beauty Chocotini
Anastasia (replaced with another)
Apple Pie
Banana Martini
Becco Martini
Black Martini
Blanch DuBois
Bloodhound
Blue Lizard Martini
Blue Monday
Cajun Combustion Engine
Capatin Lambchop
Chicago Blue
Chicago Nights
Chocolate Kiss
Chocolate-Tini
Double Chocolate Martini
Elegant
Georgian Twist
Gilligan's Island
Glacier Blue
Gotham
Jack Horner
Kiev Spring
L'Orangerie
Lava Lamp
Mandarin Martini
Mansion Martini
Martini Navratilova
Mezcatini
Mikahil's Martini
Mixed Chocolate/Chocolate Swirl
Noonday Sun
Muscovy Martini
Nashville
Natasha Rambovna
North Beach
Northwest Sunset
Nureyev
Olympic Gold
Orange Flower
Orange Lava Lamp

Orange Magnet
Patricia Petrosk
Petrograd
Purple Haze
Red Skyy
Sakuratini
Siberian Express
Spicy Hamilton
Spider Bite
Tequini
The 180
The Dreamsicle
The Inferno
The Squeeze
True North
Vladivostok

If you happen to have served any of these to guests, please extend our apologies to them and let them know it's now safe to come for drinks again.

(Regarding the Lava Lamp. This abomination, which flawlessly re-created the inaction of a lava lamp switched off and left in the garage for a few months in the dead of an Icelandic winter, somehow dodged our editorial cuts in the first edition. Once, yes. But not twice. Good-bye, Lava Lamp!)

HANGOVERS, PART ONE: PREVENTATIVES

We've divided this topic into three logical portions: what you can do before you drink and while you're drinking, what to do if you arrive home drunk, and if you wake up with a hangover.

Ever been told you should eat bread or pasta because it'll soak up the alcohol? Or perhaps the advice was to drink milk or consume fat, it'll coat your stomach and prevent undue absorption. One journalist we know drank a cup of olive oil before a night out. We're sure it kept his coat shiny (that's what our cat's vet says), but even if it did work, personally we'd rather have the hangover. If you're going to try the oil trick, at least dip bread in it. Truth is, any food slows down alcohol absorption in your system, so a big meal helps. But nothing stops it. There is a sure way to reduce the absorption of alcohol. Drink less. At a party? In dire straits? Lose your drinks halfway through each one. The bottom half is never quite as good as the top anyway. Avoid sugary drinks, which isn't hard if you're sticking to Martinis. Avoid wine when drinking cocktails as it has all the congeners that were removed from the spirits through distillation (Jared's Achilles' heel is a glass of champagne late in the evening after a few Martinis). Also, be sure to drink water when you're drinking cocktails. One junior congressman orders his Martini on the rocks and then keeps it topped up with ice and water, leaving the olive in place. A Martini or a few over the course of an enjoyable evening can be very pleasant. Too many Martinis is rarely pleasant. If it's too late to talk about moderation, proceed to Hangovers, Part Two (page 156).

GARDEN OF EDEN
FRUIT MARTINIS

Proponents of this Martini Renaissance have enriched our treasury of folklore, enhanced our mixing rituals, and challenged Luddites—er, purists—who refuse to accept the drink's inevitable evolution. (That camp proclaims that the cornucopia of modern fruit-bearing variations aren't even remote Martini cousins.) But that's like comparing a Serengeti elephant to an Ice Age woolly mammoth. The evolution is pretty obvious. Strangely, no one denies that the sweet, gomme-syruped, orange-bittered 1:1 Martini was the great-grandparent of the 4:1 and 10:1 Dry Martini.

We personally take a fully Darwinian view of the Martini. Just as it never followed one simple recipe and has changed over time, the Martini is still changing. And the name? Well, we all consider the Martini a cocktail, and everyone knows that "cocktail" is a broad term encompassing innumerable drinks. Yet, at one time there were purists steaming in their real cocktails, made with gin, bitters, sugar, and water, that nothing else was a cocktail dammit! We believe in the preservation of the Dry Martini and its classic family, but we're certainly not going to wince at any of these innovative mixes either like some die-hard classicists do.

NICK CHARLES:
Barkeeper, bring Mrs. Charles 240 Martinis. We won't be long.

—*Shadow of the Thin Man* (1941)

LOLA

CREATED BY LOREN DUNSWORTH AT DELILAH'S, VANCOUVER

Let stand

2 oz. (60 ml)
Absolut vodka

1 splash each of:
fresh orange juice, fresh grapefruit
juice, and Cointreau

orange wedge

Gin can be used in place of
vodka.

BIG BILL BARTON:
What are you calling up that
shyster for?

TIRA:
Because he helped me beat one
rap and he can do it again.

BIG BILL BARTON:
How are you mixed up in all
of this?

TIRA:
Like an olive in a Dry Martini.

—Mae West,
I'm No Angel (1933)

Once upon a time, there was a decadent little bar-restaurant nestled into the ground floor of the Buchan Hotel on Haro Street in Vancouver's West End. Delilah's was its name. It opened in the 1970s and besides offering a scrumptious menu of Pacific Northwest cuisine, this tiny jewel offered a "Martini" menu built up by its head bartender, Lola (née: Loren Dunsworth) after she arrived behind the stick in 1988.

We could break into a lounge mix of the Kinks' 1960s hit, but we won't. We'll just say that Lola divined a fabulous array of concoctions comprised of no more than two to three ingredients and shaken, stirred, or allowed to stand, then simply garnished.

It was 1995 when we first met her. We sampled a few of her creations and were immediately entranced. That Halloween night, we launched our first Web site, Shaken Not Stirred®: A Celebration of the Martini. We featured a few dozen of Lola's concoctions.

Delilah's had twelve Martinis on the menu when Lola arrived. By the time she left to open Lola's at Century House, in 1995, the list was sixty drinks strong and the back bar featured an assortment of infusion jars filled with cranberries and other fresh fruit resting in vodka.

As we now realize, Lola pioneered the first Martini menu back in those early days. It was a landmark in the Martini Renaissance, although few people outside of the Pacific Northwest knew it.

"When we opened Lola's at Century House, Marion [her partner at the time] and I knew that we had to create our own

Martini and champagne cocktail list," Lola recalled. She formulated an avant range of gin- and vodka-based Martinis, which were presented in the single-serving three-part shakers she made them in, accompanied by frosty cocktail glasses.

Professional female mixologists like Lola came into their own during the 1990s. As Lola herself casually remarked: "Women are super-tasters. It's in their makeup to be more orally sensitive to tastes and textures. They can detect subtle differences."

That talent has certainly earned Lola a place in the Martini Mixologists' Hall of Fame, which we will explain in a bit.

We will never forget those early days with Lola, especially that last New Year's Eve, in 1996, at Lola's at Century House.

The sumptuous meal was only the first course. Modern Martinis flowed like water from the center-stage bar where Lola—dressed in a silver lamé Patti LaBelle jumpsuit with big shoulders—dispensed her creations. The invitation-only guests conga-lined late into the night before making our way to the various corners of Vancouver that we all called home.

Then Lola disappeared from sight. But then so did we as we made our way down south to San Francisco and Idaho before the year was out to drink a lot of gin in the former and in the latter work as gin tasters for the United States's first post-Prohibition microdistillery restaurant—the Bardenay.

Where was Lola? It took us a while to discover the truth of our favorite bartender's disappearance—but most of you heard about it before we did.

The Lola can also be served as a dinner finale. Lola's served a **Lola Granitée**. Combine all the ingredients in a glass or metal bowl and place it in the freezer hours ahead of time. Every twenty minutes or so, use a fork to break up and stir any ice that forms. Do it quickly and put it right back in the freezer so it doesn't melt. You should end up with a sorbet consistency. When it's all frozen, you don't have to stir it any more, and it'll keep for a few days. If it doesn't freeze at all, try again using less alcohol and more juice. Once it is frozen, you can add a touch more spirit, if it was also kept in the freezer.

APPLETINI

CREATED AT LOLA'S, WEST HOLLYWOOD

Shake

1.5 oz. (45 ml)
Ketel One vodka

1.5 oz. (45 ml)
DeKuyper Sour Apple Pucker

1 splash sweet & sour mix

slice of Granny Smith apple
marinated in lemon water

Many have attempted
to lay claim to this but
DeKuyper—the makers of
the apple pucker liquor—
will attest to the fact that
Lola's is where it all began.

—Loren Dunsworth, in
an interview, 2011

You lose track of people when you live in the fast lane on the spirituous road. Lola was one of the people who took that freeway down south and disappeared off our radar for years. Yet we remember that the first apple-based Martini we ever had was crafted by her masterful hands.

Called the William Tell, she convinced us back in 1995 that apples could a Martini make. After that experience, we briefly tried an apple Martini like the William Tell or the Palace Apple Skyy a day, but our neighborhood doctor kept showing up (turned out he loved them, too).

Lola can be lauded for being sensitive to what the public wants. When she moved to Hollywood, in 1996, she knew that her guests had a sweet tooth. She did what any great bartender does. She catered to their caprices.

When she opened Lola's on North Fairfax in West Hollywood, her opening barman Adam came up with the Appletini—called Adam's Apple, at the time. People loved it. When she tried to replace it with another drink, her guests retaliated. Six months later, the Appletini went back on the menu and is still her best seller to this day—twenty thousand Appletinis are shaken at Lola's every month.

Queen of the first Martini menu, champion of the Appletini, we are so happy that we met Lola back in the day, when Delilah's was the stage that she played like a violin, and even happier we've found her again.

When Lola was at Delilah's she mixed the **William Tell**, shaking 2 oz. (60 ml) Stolichnaya vodka, 1 splash pressed apple juice, and 1 splash Rose's Lime Cordial.

Lola's **Red Caramel Apple Martini** puts a twist on her famed drink, shaking 1 oz. (30 ml) Ketel One vodka, 1 oz. (30 ml) DeKuyper Sour Apple Pucker, 0.5 oz. (15 ml) butterscotch liqueur, and 1 splash cranberry juice.

Seattle's Palace Kitchen made a **Palace Apple Skyy**, shaking 1.5 oz. (45 ml) Skyy vodka, 0.5 oz. (15 ml) Marie Brizard calvados, 2 drops Goldschläger, garnished with a grilled green apple slice.

Legend has it that back in the late 1970s the Ardilaun Hotel in County Galway, Ireland, served an **Ardilaun Appletini**, shaking 1.5 oz. (45 ml) Absolut vodka, 0.5 oz. (15 ml) Berentzen Apfelkorn schnapps, and 0.5 oz. (15 ml) Cointreau.

While living in New York, we came up with our own **Golden Apple Martini**, shaking 1.5 oz. (45 ml) Ketel One vodka, 0.75 oz. (20 ml) Berentzen Apfelkorn schnapps, 0.5 oz. (15 ml) fresh sour mix, garnishing the glass with a cinnamon sugar rim.

Michael Waterhouse of Dylan Prime divined a "pietini" called **Apple Pie à la Mode**, shaking 0.5 oz. (15 ml) Licor 43 and 1 oz. (30 ml) whipping cream until thick. Set aside. In a fresh mixing glass, shake 1 oz. (30 ml) Absolut vodka, 1 oz. (30 ml) apple schnapps, and 1 oz. (30 ml) pure maple syrup. Garnish with the thickened cream.

Another great bartender and dear friend (yes, Mom, I'm known to and friends with bartenders around the world), Nick Strangeway, took us to meet Dick Bradsell when he was still behind the bar at the Colony Room, a hole-in-the-wall private London club with a Who's Who's of British art and theater as members. There was Mr. Bradsell, inventor of the Bramble, Cowboy Hoof Martini, Detroit Martini, Pharmaceutical Stimlulant . . . "What can I get you?" he asked. I replied for all of us, "Whatever you feel like making." A few minutes later, he arrived with what he, an overworked bartender, felt like making on a busy night: a round of gin and tonics.

FRESH FRUIT MARTINI

CREATED BY DICK BRADSELL, LONDON

Shake

1.5 oz. (45 ml)
Absolut vodka

0.75 oz. (20 ml)
crushed fruit or fruit purée

1 splash
sugar syrup (optional)

fresh fruit

To remove as much pulp as
possible, double strain the drink
using both a hawthorn strainer
on the mixing glass and a tea
strainer over the cocktail glass.

One [Martini] is all right,
two is too many, and three
is not enough.

—James Thurber

When we first launched our Web site, Shaken Not Stirred, back in 1995, no one had conceived of making a Martini with fresh fruit. Fruit juice, yes. But fresh fruit?

But then we hadn't met London legend Dick Bradsell yet, who did just that after tasting a Black Martini at the Fifty-Seven Fifty-Seven Bar in New York's Four Seasons Hotel during a 1995 bartender fam trip. He divined a version made with fresh, seasonal fruits.

A symphony of simplicity and seasonality, you may know Dick's Fresh Fruit Martini under its various seasonal names: Raspberry Martini, Watermelon Martini, Strawberry Martini, keep going.

Maybe we get a little more obsessed than most with this recipe. We planted blackcurrants, strawberries, cape gooseberries, cherries, and raspberries in our vegetable garden and we forage the hedgerows behind the house for blackberries, quince, sloe berries, and damsons every year. Our local farmers' markets offer up a variety of apples and pears. It's one of the more entertaining ways to get part of our five-a-day.

This bounty doesn't stop us from foraging at the supermarket for pineapples, mangoes, passionfruit, kiwi fruit, and papayas when the mood strikes. Neither does it stop us from buying packaged fruit purées from Boiron and Funkin when we want to serve up rounds of Lychee Martinis. (Don't know about you, but the results of making a Lychee Martini with the syrup from canned lychees are equal to biting down hard on a rusty Phillips head.)

The only fruit that we haven't heard anyone use to make one of Dick's Fresh Fruit Martinis is durian. But then what can you do with a fruit that you have to hold out the car window while you transport it home and keep the windows opened in the kitchen when you cut it open.

Fifty-Seven Fifty-Seven's **Black Martini** shook 3 oz. (90 ml) vodka and 0.5 oz. (15 ml) Chambord.

Kittichai in New York serves up a **Lychee Martini** that purées 10 canned lychees in a blender with 1 oz. (30 ml) sugar syrup, and 0.5 oz. (15 ml) fresh lemon juice. Pour the mixture into a mixing glass and shake with 1 oz. Skyy vodka, and 0.5 oz. (15 ml) Cointreau.

A simplification of Kittichai's excellent Lychee Martini, our **Lychee Martini #2**, shakes up 2 oz. (60ml) Absolut vodka with 1.5 oz. (45 ml) Funkin lychee purée and 1 splash Cointreau.

Bradsell's classic **Watermelon Martini** muddles 1 slice fresh watermelon (from a melon cut into 16 sections) into a mixing glass and shakes it with 2 oz. (60 ml) Absolut vodka and 0.5 oz. (15 ml) sugar syrup.

Bradsell's original **Raspberry Martini** shakes 1.5 oz. (45 ml) Absolut vodka, 1 oz. (30 ml) raspberry purée, 0.5 (15 ml) raspberry liqueur, 0.25 oz. (5 ml) sugar syrup, and 1 splash fresh lime juice, garnished with a fresh raspberry.

The **Classic Bloodhound** from the 1930s mixes 1 oz. (30 ml) French vermouth, 1 oz. (30 ml) Italian vermouth, 1 oz. (30 ml) Plymouth gin, garnished with a fresh, whole strawberry. Later versions also included 1 splash strawberry liqueur. These days, you can replace that with a splash of strawberry purée or muddle 2 whole strawberries into the mixing glass.

COSMOPOLITAN

CREDITED TO CHERYL COOK AND OTHERS

Shake

1.5 oz. (45 ml)
Absolut Citron

0.75 oz. (20 ml)
cranberry juice cocktail

0.5 ml (15 ml) Cointreau

1 splash fresh lime juice

flamed orange twist

Don't make this drink with super-strength cranberry juice from the natural food store. Your cheeks will disappear into your teeth from the tartness.

"Cranberry juice. It just occurs to me. How would vodka go with that?"

—Richard Nixon on the campaign trail in 1959, speaking at the Wisconsin cranberry center

Yes, it's got color, it's got taste. It's got about as many reputed creators as the Martini itself. Pretty and pink, the Cosmopolitan swept across Miami's South Beach, San Francisco fern bars, Vancouver, and New York's TriBeCa and Midtown. Each place claims to have invented it or improved it. What is certain is that two people popularized it back in the late 1980s and the hit TV series *Sex and the City* cemented it on the global radar.

The Cosmopolitan was only one in a long line of drinks that paired vodka and cranberry juice. Take a look at the Cosmopolitan time line:

1951: Trader Vic's Cranberry Christmas punch hits the papers with vodka, cranberry juice, Rose's Lime Juice, water, and sugar. Later, Trader Vic's offers a Cape Codder #1 in an old-fashioned glass and a Cape Codder #2 as a highball topped with soda.

1960: A bar on Hollywood's Sunset Strip is serving the Santa Baby cocktail—vodka and cranberry—at Christmastime.

1963: Ocean Spray Cranberry Juice teamed up with Don Cossack Vodka and launched Tropico Sea Breeze in bottles, to be served on the rocks and up as a cocktail.

1975: Neal Murray at the Cork & Cleaver Steakhouse in Minneapolis claims that he invented the Cosmopolitan, inspired by the idea of putting cranberry juice into a Kamikaze.

1978: John Parks at the Tropical Pub in Belmar, New Jersey, creates the Woo Woo.

1979: The Kamikaze first makes its appearance in bars across the United States.

1985/1986: Cheryl Cook at the Strand in South Beach, Miami, makes a Kamikaze with "Absolut Citron, a splash of triple sec, a drop of Rose's Lime Juice and just enough cranberry to make it oh so pretty in pink." (Note: Absolut launched Absolut Citron in 1988.)

1987: Melissa Huffsmith at the Odeon in New York takes a recipe that her friend Patrick Mullen had tried in Miami using plain Absolut. Along with Toby Cecchini she comes up with a Cosmopolitan, using Absolut Citron, Cointreau, fresh lime juice, and cranberry juice.

1988/1989: Lola at Delilah's in Vancouver puts a Cosmopolitan and a Metropolitan on her Martini menu.

1996: Dale DeGroff at the Rainbow Room refines the Cosmopolitan recipe and introduces it to Madonna.

1998: The Cosmopolitan appears in episodes of the *Sex and the City* TV series.

You just can't keep a good cocktail from being invented and reinvented and enhanced. Look at the Martini. Look at the Cosmo.

We have another story to tell about the Cosmopolitan.

Every January, from 2002 until 2010, we got together with a group of friends out in the British countryside for a weekend of cooking and drinks mixing. (Helps when 85 percent of your friends are chefs and bartenders.) The locations were carefully chosen: a Gothic folly on the grounds of the Stowe School, where Richard Branson and Christopher Milne (of Winnie-the-Pooh fame) spent their formative years, and the orangery on the Frampton Court Estate.

Cheryl Cook's **Cosmopolitan** shook 2 oz. (60 ml) Absolut Citron, 1 splash triple sec, drops of Rose's Lime Cordial, and just enough cranberry juice to make it pink.

Mellisa Huffman and Toby Cecchini at the Odeon's **Cosmopolitan** shook 2 oz. (60 ml) Absolut Citron, 1.5 oz. (45 ml) cranberry juice cocktail, 0.75 oz. fresh lime juice, 0.75 oz. Cointreau.

Dale DeGroff's **Cosmopolitan** shakes 1.5 oz. (45 ml) Absolut Citron, 1 oz. (30 ml) cranberry juice cocktail, 0.5 oz. (15 ml) Cointreau, 1 splash fresh lime juice, garnished with a flamed orange twist.

Loren Dunsworth's **Cosmopolitan** at Delilah's shook 2 oz. (60 ml) Stolichnaya Vodka, 1 splash cranberry juice cocktail, 1 splash Rose's Lime Cordial, and 1 dash Cointreau.

When Ben Reed was at London's Met Hotel, he created the **Metropolitan**, shaking 1.5 oz. (45 ml) Absolut Kurant, 1 oz. (30 ml) cranberry juice cocktail, 0.75 oz. (20 ml) Cointreau, and 0.75 oz. (20 ml) fresh lime juice, garnished with a flamed orange twist.

The Chateau Marmont's Bar Marmont made its **Cosmopolitan** shaking 3 oz. (90 ml) cranberry-infused vodka (see Infused Spirits on page 193), 0.5 oz. (15 ml) triple sec, 1 splash Rose's Lime Cordial, garnished with a maraschino cherry.

The **Kamikaze Cocktail** shakes 1.5 oz. (45 ml) Absolut vodka, 1 oz. (30 ml) Cointreau, and 1 oz. (30 ml) fresh lime juice, garnished with a lime wedge.

The **Woo Woo** built 2 oz. (60 ml) vodka, 2.5 oz. (75 ml) cranberry juice cocktail, and 0.5 oz. (15 ml) peach schnapps in an ice-filled highball glass.

The 1933 **Cosmopolitan Daisy** shakes 2 oz. (60 ml) Beefeater gin, 1 oz. (30 ml) fresh raspberry syrup, 0.5 oz. (15 ml) triple sec, and 0.5 oz. (15 ml) fresh lime juice. (See page 197 for fresh raspberry syrup recipe.)

Angus Winchester commemorated the full solar eclipse that was seen in Britain on August 11, 1999, by creating an **Eclipse Martini**, shaking 1 oz. (30 ml) dry gin, 1 oz. (30 ml) cranberry juice, 0.5 oz. (15 ml) blue curaçao, 1 dash peach schnapps.

January 2007 was an exceptional year. We took over the entire Old Campden House estate in Chipping Campden, Gloucestershire: two banqueting houses, an almonry, and a gate house that surrounded the ruins of the original manor that was destroyed, in 1645, by a fire. The assembled weekenders included Robert "Drinkboy" Hess, London master mixologists Nick Strangeway and Dré Masso, Nick Blacknell of Beefeater Gin, and Sasha Petraske from Milk & Honey.

We had just been on a major archeological excavation of the New York Public Library and had found a series of tiny volumes printed in 1933 titled *Pioneers of Mixing Gins at Elite Bars*. One page stopped us in our tracks when we found a Cosmopolitan Daisy, made with gin, raspberry syrup, lemon juice, and Cointreau. Along with an Elizabethan recipe for spice-crusted, slow-roasted beef brisket and a Victorian recipe for roasted goose with autumn fruits, the Cosmopolitan Daisy was our contribution to the weekend feast.

Fresh raspberries were a cinch to come by at the market (not local, sadly). So a simmering pot of fresh raspberry syrup greeted diners as they arrived in the West Banqueting House.

Eyes opened wide and anticipatory noises were heard from every corner.

The ultimate test came in June that same year when we threw an after-party on the closing day of the London Bar Show at our house in West Ealing. This time, all of the assembled took turns making drinks: gaz regan, Robert Hess, Charles Vexenat, Dré Masso, Henry Besant, Julio Bermejo, Nick Strangeway, and Dick Bradsell. As sips shaken from large antique cocktail shakers were tested, gestures of approval or

dismay circulated from the kitchen to the dining room. Occasionally, we would hear Dick make the comment: "Interesting." (He took us aside and whispered that he makes that comment when he doesn't like something, but uses it as a cordial escape.)

When we shook up our 1933 Cosmopolitan Daisy, all he said was: "Now that's a damned good drink!"

When we found the 1933 recipe, the cocktail chat rooms were buzzing, but the news didn't come from us. A German bartender, Jöerg Meyer, had sent a donation to our Web site's cocktail fund, then thought he'd peek to see if we used the account's data storage, as there were no passwords on them at that time. It was like Aladdin's cave. There were all the cocktail books we'd photographed and scanned, including *Pioneers*. Reading it cover to cover, our now dear friend landed on the Cosmopolitan Daisy, mixed it, loved it, and sent it out into the world.

Is the modern Cosmo descended from this 1933 recipe? While it is possible, it is far more likely this is one of those rare cosmic coincidences—two drinks with remarkably similar ingredients, similar flavor, and the same name but invented in different eras by bartenders with no knowledge of each other, leaving us blissfully spoiled for choice, which is all that really matters in the end.

PUMPKIN MARTINI

CREATED BY LOREN DUNSWORTH AT LOLA'S, HOLLYWOOD

Don't you agree that sometimes a dessert in a glass is far more alluring than a slab of pie à la mode or a whole sundae, especially when you're on a hot date and don't want to look like you're troughing? Call them what you will—Caketails and Pietinis, trademarked by Michael Waterhouse, or Dessert Martinis as Lola calls them—are creative and luscious.

Over the past ten years, we've sampled our way through Key Lime Pie, Lemon Meringue, and Pumpkin Martinis without ever feeling that we need to run to the gym for an emergency calorie burn. Without fail, we achieved a blissful sense of the meal's completion from a single glass. But isn't that what we all want after dinner—a little something sweet and satisfying?

Shake

2 oz. (60 ml) Captain Morgan Original Spiced Rum

1 oz. (30 ml) Bols Pumpkin Smash Liqueur

0.5 oz. (15 ml) heavy cream

1 heaping spoonful pumpkin pie filling

grating of nutmeg

LEMON DROP

CREATED AT HENRY AFRICA'S, SAN FRANCISCO

Shake

1.5 oz. (45 ml) vodka

1 oz. (30 ml) fresh lemon juice

0.5 oz. (15 ml) triple sec

1 dash sugar syrup

prepare a chilled cocktail glass with
a sugar rim

When the shadow of the grasshopper falls across the trail of the field mouse on the green and slimy grass as a red sun rises above the western horizon silhouetting a gaunt and tautly muscled Indian warrior perched with bow and arrow cocked and aimed straight at you it's time for another Martini.

—An anonymous passage
written on the mural
outside Vesuvio's Café
in San Francisco, CA

San Francisco fern bars during the 1970s were as classy a place to find your next love as you could imagine in the early disco era. Henry Africa's was probably the most famous of the lot back in the day. Brass, wood, stained glass, Tiffany lamps, hanging plants, and ferns, of course, served as backdrops for sipping Lemon Drops and telling the person next to you that you could guess his/her astrological sign in under twelve tries.

Well, Henry Africa's is no longer, yet the Lemon Drop lives on even though it has evolved alongside cocktail culture over the past forty years. Like its kissing cousins the Kamikaze and the Cosmopolitan, its appeal lies in its citrusy taste and aroma.

Taking advantage of today's availablity of citron vodkas, the **Lemon Drop #2** shakes 1.5 oz. (45ml) Absolut Citron, 0.75 oz. (25 ml) fresh lemon juice, and 0.5 oz. (15 ml) sugar syrup, garnished with a lemon twist.

A traditional Italian liquor that's made as often at home as it is purchased, limoncello is used to make **Lemon Drop #3**, shaking 1.5 oz. (45ml) Absolut Citron and 0.5 oz. (15 ml) limoncello, strained into a sugar-rimmed cocktail glass.

PORN STAR MARTINI

CREATED BY DOUGLAS ANKRAH AT TOWNHOUSE, LONDON

There's something sexy about a Martini: The shape of the glass, whether you call it a cocktail glass or a Martini glass, commands respect with an unstated note of passion and sensuous pleasure.

One of the founders of the London Academy of Bartenders (LAB), Douglas Ankrah, came up with a Martini that says it all—the Porn Star Martini—when he developed the cocktail menu for Townhouse in London's Knightsbridge district.

When we first encountered the Porn Star at Townhouse, we knew what the titillation was all about: half a fresh passionfruit sprinkled with vanilla sugar and a tall shot of brut champagne accompanied the smooth-textured Martini.

Douglas's drink has been replicated on most continents because it says everything one would expect in a chilled stemmed cocktail glass.

Shake

1.75 oz. (50 ml)
Cariel Vanilla vodka

0.75 oz. (20 ml)
passionfruit juice

1 splash
passionfruit syrup

half a fresh passionfruit sprinkled with vanilla sugar and a shot glass filled with brut champagne

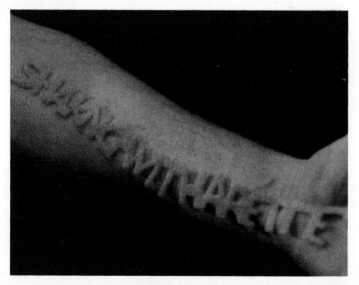

CHOCOLATE, COFFEE & FLOWERS

DESSERT MARTINIS

Flowers, chocolate, coffee, enticing cocktails: These are the essences of romance. A magazine survey once asked its readers: "Is chocolate better than sex?" We say, Why choose one or the other! Chocolate Martinis are a bit of both, nicely mixed and served chilled.

Why make a Chocolate Martini when there are other cocoa-based drinks out there? Because these are rich without being sugary, they have the relaxing effect of a classic Martini, and when you first try them, they're an incredible surprise.

Coffee has become chocolate's second in command thanks to Mochachinos, White Chocolate Lattes, and other comfort coffees that have fueled the Naughties. The Martinis were there first.

Flower garnishes make a real statement: whether you're celebrating the rites of spring, or just broadcasting the intensity of your midwinter cabin fever. And if the night calls for sheets scattered with rose petals, there's nothing like a few matching Martinis to set the mood.

If you've never munched on nasturtium blossoms or rose petals, you're in for a surprise. Most of the edible varieties have a tangy edge that's perfect in a Martini. Tip: Buy unsprayed, organic flowers or look for edible flowers in the produce section.

I'm angry. Somebody slipped a brown Martini in on me. Perhaps it's that sappy bartender using mascara again.

—Ernie Kovacs
(as Percy Dovetonsils)

HANGOVERS, PART TWO: PREVENTATIVES

You overdid it, but you've made it home safe and sound. There are a few things you can do before you go to sleep (or pass out). Take two aspirin and drink a pint or two of orange juice. One probable cause of post-Bacchanalian distress is a constriction of blood vessels in the brain; aspirin is a mild vasodilator. One other problem stems from severe dehydration. Alcohol actually sucks liquid out of your system, and orange juice replenishes it.

Take a multivitamin. It's rumored that vitamin B depletion contributes to the brain damage found in career drinkers. Things looking bleak? You might have to purge. There's still a bunch of alcohol in your stomach. Better now than in the morning.

PERCY DOVETONSILS

INSPIRED BY AN ERNIE KOVACS CHARACTER

"Greetings from your orthocon tube," Percy Dovetonsils chimed at the opening of *The Ernie Kovacs Show* during the late 1950s and early 1960s. Wearing a tiger-skin print satin smoking jacket with black velvet lapels and cuffs, a silk ascot aound his neck, and sipping a Martini garnished with an olive attached to a fresh daisy, Dovetonsils was an inspiration for modern-day lounge lizards.

Most baby boomers discovered the euphoric effects of Martinis while observing their parents at cocktail parties. Anistatia confesses that Ernie Kovacs and his weekly television broadcasts raised her curiosity about potent potables. Kovacs's self-proclaimed poet laureate opened his segment by taking a sip, nibbling the olive, and making a simple comment such as:

> Actually, these Martinis that I drink are particularly wonderful because there's a very attractive young lady here in the studio who dips her little finger in it each time. Too bad she doesn't trim her nails.

Other times, his salutation would be a little more involved:

> Greetings. Greetings indeed. There has been some talk that I'm drinking real gin in this glass for my Martini. I objurgate such talk. It's not gin. It's a phony prop. It's white scotch. Besides, last week I had to join AA to continue in this spot. I did. It's Albert Alexander's bar. It's a wonderful little place.

Shake

2 oz. (60 ml)
Beefeater London Dry Gin

1 oz. (30 ml)
fresh lemon juice

1 dash
grenadine syrup

a fresh daisy

(See fresh and preserved flower petal garnish instructions on page 198.)

I complained about the daisy [in my Martini] being unreal the other day. [Now] they have a real daisy in here, real gin in here, and a real stuffed olive. Only the pimento is plastic.

—Ernie Kovacs
(as Percy Dovetonsils)

The Provençale served at New York's Employee's Only is the ultimate floral Martini experience, stirring 2 oz. (60 ml) Employees Only Lavender-infused Gin, 1.25 oz. Employees Only Vermouth de Provence, 0.75 oz. Cointreau, garnished with an orange twist.

(For the lavender-infused gin and Vermouth de Provence recipes, see pages 195, 196.)

Alessandro Palazzi at Dukes Hotel in London paid homage to Ian Fleming and his favorite fragrance, Floris No. 89, creating a **Fleming 89 Martini** that builds in a frozen glass a Fortnum & Mason candied rose, 1 drop chocolate bitters, 1 dash rose liqueur, 0.5 oz. (15 ml) tonka bean-infused vodka, 1 oz. (30 ml) Stolichnaya Elit vodka, and 0.5 oz. (15 ml) proprietary amber vermouth.

Seeing this happy tippler sitting on a swing, playing a piano, or reciting one of his immortal odes to bookworms, fad diets, or other inconsequential anomalies (which went right over her preadolescent head) while sipping a Martini was probably the biggest influence on Anistatia's adult drinking habits. Cigar-smoking Kovacs also elevated her appreciation of music, playing excerpts from Kurt Weill's *Threepenny Opera* and Juan García Esquivel hits like "Sentimental Journey" and "Mucha Muchacha."

A few years later, Kovacs and Dovetonsils were no more. They were quickly replaced by an undying infatuation with Sean Connery and his super spy character, James Bond. It took a few decades of Martini consumption before she learned the comprehensive subtlety one can achieve from sipping the elixir: While watching a Kovacs retrospective, we *finally* noticed that Whistler's mother was riding a Harley in the painting behind Percy Dovetonsils!

We digress. As Dovetonsils commented in his last show: "I think I know where that extra bottle of Martinis went that I had here, it's up in the control room."

The Fawlty Flower made at Delilah's mixed 2 oz. (60 ml) vodka and 1 splash fresh lime juice. Preserved flower petals were floated on top. (See fresh and preserved flower petal garnish instructions on page 198.)

The **Violet Martini** shakes 1.5 oz. (45 ml) Hendrick's gin, 0.75 oz. (20 ml) Bitter Truth Violet Liqueur or Giffard Crème de Violette, 0.75 oz. (20 ml) rosé champagne, 1 splash vanilla-infused gomme syrup.

THE 911

CREATED BY LOLA OF LOLA'S AT CENTURY HOUSE, VANCOUVER

You've all heard the plaintive cry of a chocoholic in midafternoon withdrawal crying, "I need an emergency chocolate fix." You've watched the poor creature salivate at the sight of a giant Toblerone bar or experience orgasmic satisfaction with the first bite of a hand-rolled chocolate truffle.

Well, some of these wanton souls are also Martini drinkers. We really hadn't experienced the addictive nature of a chocolate Martini until we dined one evening at Lola's and stimulated our appetites with the 911. Then we understood. We got around to ordering duck confit and perfectly grilled lamb chops a few drinks later.

Purists might feel that a Chocolate Martini chilled in the very shaker that caresses their classic blend is sacrilegious. But chocolate—like Martinis, music, and memorable romantic companions—is a seductively sensual treat. So why not combine two enchanting excesses in a shaker while listening to the third, and eventually sharing it with a fourth?

On the set of the 1956 hit film *Giant,* Liz Taylor and Rock Hudson spent a lot of time drinking together. "During our toots we created the best drink I ever tasted," Taylor recalled, "a Chocolate Martini made with vodka, Hershey's syrup and Kahlúa." Considering how she and their co-star James Dean fought on set, it's hard to say if he was invited to join them.

Then we learned of the Tootsie Roll Martini from a Chicago connoisseur, Jerry Langland, who also introduced us to the Hershey's Kiss. Guess what the garnish is. (Maybe it's the aroma of Milk Duds waft-

Let stand

2 oz. (60 ml)
Stolichnaya vodka

1 splash
Godiva Chocolate Liqueur

1 splash
fresh raspberry pureé

fresh raspberry

So what do you serve with a Chocolate Martini? Try a plate of strawberries with the tops trimmed off, surrounding a dish of Godiva chocolates. To brighten the flavor of the berries, stand them cut side down in a tablespoon or two of balsamic vinegar. (If you're skeptical, try it on a single berry first. We served them that way to the general manager of a luxury hotel. His reaction: "Where'd you find such perfect strawberries at this time of year?") A pinch of fresh ground black pepper further accentuates their flavor. Or you can macerate them in a little triple sec or Lillet Blanc.

Hidetsugu Ueno of Bar High Five wanted to make a **Real Chocolate Martini** without melting chocolate into vodka, so he stirs 1.5 oz. (45 ml) Mozart Dry and 1 tsp. (5 ml) Mozart Black in a mixing glass coated with 4 atomizer sprays of Martini Bianco over the ice.

Elizabeth Taylor's **Chocolate Martini** shakes 2 oz. (60 ml) vodka and 1 oz. (30 ml) Kahlúa. Drizzle Hershey's syrup around the inside of the cocktail glass before straining the mixture into it.

ing from the Holloway Candy Company production plant near the downtown area that's inspired everyone to order chocolate-laced drinks.)

Mint is one of chocolate's long-standing companions. Lust for the flavor of an After Eight or the ubiquitous Girl Scout treat? The Thin Mint Martini beckons.

Back in New York, the final encounter occurred at Dylan Prime, where Michael Waterhouse crafted a series of Caketails and Pietinis. One of his crowning glories still lingers on our palates, the German Chocolate Caketini.

Jerry Langland's **Tootsie Roll Martini** shakes 1 oz. (30 ml) Stolichnaya vodka, 1 oz. (30 ml) Godiva Chocolate Liqueur, and 1 splash Grand Marnier, garnished with an orange slice.

Set 'Em Up Joe's **Hershey's Kiss** combined 2 oz. (60 ml) Wyborowka vodka, 0.5 oz. (15 ml) Bols Dark Crème de Cacao, 1 dash heavy cream, and a Hershey's Chocolate Kiss garnish.

Our **Thin Mint** shakes 1.5 oz. (45 ml) Ketel One Vodka, 0.75 oz. (20 ml) dark chocolate liqueur, and 0.75 oz. (20 ml) white crème de menthe.

Michael Waterhouse, formerly of Dylan Prime in New York, made a **German Chocolate Caketini**, shaking 1.5 oz. (45 ml) dark chocolate liqueur, 1 oz. (30 ml) Absolut Vodka, 1 oz. (30 ml) Malibu Rum, 1 splash caramel liqueur, and 1 splash hazelnut liqueur. In a separate mixing glass, shake 3 oz. (90 ml) whipping cream and 1 oz. (30 ml) chocolate syrup. Float on top.

VODKA ESPRESSO

CREATED BY DICK BRADSELL AT FRED'S PLACE, LONDON

Can a simple drink have legs that span a few decades and stretch around the globe? Yes.

Some say Dick Bradsell first created the Vodka Espresso when he was behind the bar, in 1983, at the Soho Brasserie. Others say that it was created a year later when he headed the bar at the raucous members' club Fred's Place. This was the establishment in which—legend has it—a model walked into the club and asked Bradsell to make a drink that would "wake me up and %@&# me up." He shook Italian espresso hard and fast with coffee liqueur and Absolut vodka.

The resulting libation not only kept this unnamed beauty happy and awake throughout her night out, it became the preferred drink of the Fred's Place bar both during and after hours.

This concoction was made even more stimulating, in 1998, when Bradsell crafted the cocktail menu for artist Damien Hirst's Notting Hill Gate restaurant, Pharmacy. The list of drinks was inspired by the drink names that Hirst gave Bradsell. It seems pretty obvious in hindsight why the enhanced Vodka Espresso was named the Pharmaceutical Stimulant. With two types of coffee liqueur—one sweeter and one more intensely coffee flavored—the drink never needed the addition of sugar or sugar syrup as some would have you believe.

The American palate leans more toward softer cappuccinos and lattes than unapologetic espresso. So, around 2004, legendary American mixologist Dale

Shake

2 oz. (60 ml) Absolut vodka

0.75 oz. (20 ml) Kahlúa

1.5 oz. (45 ml) espresso, cooled to room temperature

3 espresso beans

To get this drink to properly froth on top, make sure you use real espresso. Don't skimp on the shaking, either. Shake it hard until the outside of the shaker is thoroughly frosted.

We make an Irish whiskey version to give the **Irish Vodka Espresso** a touch of the mellowness found in an Irish Coffee.

Peter Jeary at the Hawksmoor at Seven Dials gives his house coffee liqueur a touch of complexity by using a high-quality mescal and agave syrup instead of sugar. It's the secret of the bar's signature Vodka Espresso variation–the **Square Mile Martini.**

(See page 194 for a basic coffee liqueur recipe.)

DeGroff devised an Espresso Martini for those who prefer cream and a touch of sugar in their coffee.

Upping the ante just once more down by New York's financial district, Dylan Prime's Michael Waterhouse added vanilla liqueur to his Espresso Martini and topped it with a scoop of French vanilla ice cream.

On the Internet, variations abound with bartenders adding Cointreau, raspberry liqueur, B&B, you name it. But then it's no surprise after peeking at the lineup of Italian syrups Starbucks offers to dose your latte.

Our personal preference—like Peter Jeary in London's Hawksmoor at Seven Dials—is to make our own coffee liqueur.

Dick Bradsell's **Pharmaceutical Stimulant** shakes 2 oz. (60 ml) Absolut vodka, 0.5 oz. (15 ml) Kahlúa, 0.5 oz. (15 ml) Tia Maria, and 1.5 oz. (45ml) cooled espresso, garnished with 3 espresso beans.

Dale DeGroff's **Espresso Martini** shakes 0.75 oz. (20 ml) Absolut vodka, 0.75 oz. (20 ml) Kahlúa, 1 oz. (30 ml) cold espresso, and 0.5 oz. (15 ml) simple syrup. Whip heavy cream without sugar ahead of time and store in the refrigerator. Rim a cocktail glass with water and granulated sugar. Let stand to harden. Strain into the prepared glass. Float the cream on top.

Michael Waterhouse's **Dylan Prime Espresso Martini** shakes 2 oz. (60 ml) cooled espresso, 1 oz. (30 ml) vodka, 1 oz. (30ml) Tia Maria, and 1.5 oz. (45 ml) Licor 43, garnished with a scoop of French vanilla ice cream.

SAKURATINI

CREATED BY SUNTORY, LIMITED

Sipping Sakuratinis in Tokyo during cherry blossom season reminded us of an art that Japan introduced to the West over five centuries ago: flower arrangement. The Japanese have no equivalent for the word "love." However, they do convey that emotion without words by sending their loved ones specific flowers arranged to convey various messages. (They even created the perfect floral "Dear John" letter: a single yellow rose sent with a mirror and a comb, which loosely means "I no longer see you behind me in the morning as I comb my hair because I have lost my love for you.")

In the West, the language of flowers is described in books like *The People's Almanac* by David Wallechinsky and Irving Wallace and *Webster's New Collegiate Dictionary*. There are even a few edible varieties with hidden meanings like nasturtiums, peach blossoms, apple blossoms, jasmine, bachelor buttons, rosemary, cherry blossoms, chrysanthemums, pansies, orange blossoms, sunflowers, clover, marigolds, zinnias, roses, and violets. Garnish your date's Martini with a secret floral message! You could say a lot over a couple of drinks without ever uttering a word.

Shake

3 oz. (90 ml)
Suntory Reserve Whisky
or Bombay Sapphire Gin

1 oz. (30 ml)
Suntory Sakura Liqueur

preserved cherry blossom

(See fresh and preserved flower petal garnish instructions on page 198.)

Say It with Flowers

We found a few edible floral garnishes that express hidden thoughts of love:

APPLE BLOSSOM:
"I prefer you."

CHRYSANTHEMUM:
(red) "I love you"; (other colors) "I feel slighted."

DAISY:
(white) "You are innocent."

PEACH BLOSSOM:
"I am your captive."

ROSE:
(deep red) "I am bashful"; (white) "I am worthy of you"; (yellow) "I'm happy to be friends."

VIOLET:
(blue) "I'm faithful to you."

Lola's **Ma Chérie** mixes 2 oz. (60 ml) sun-dried cherry vodka and 1 splash cherry brandy. (See sun-dried cherry vodka recipe on page 194.)

THE SILK ROAD
SPICED MARTINIS

Every time we sip a cinnamon-laced Martini, we remember when we were kids combing the issues of *National Geographic*. Those dreams of exotic destinations dance through our heads once again. Did you ever want to retrace the Spice Route that snaked northward from the Ivory Coast to the Casbah? Did you ever want to traverse the Silk Road, trading tea from the Far East in exchange for European almonds and other delights? Did you ever want to brave the American frontier like Jack London's get-rich-or-die-trying characters who sought their fortunes in Alaskan gold instead of cinnamon or pepper?

The secret to longevity? Never travel to any place you haven't been before, never stay up past 8 p.m., always go to bed alone, and never drink another Martini. Follow these simple rules and you still may not live forever, but it'll sure seem like forever.

HANGOVERS, PART THREE: PALLIATIVES

First, let's clear something up about the adage, "Haf a lil' hair of th' dog that bit'cha." More alcohol the morning after doesn't cure a hangover. It does postpone the inevitable (we've met a few people who've been staving off theirs for years, and believe us, it's not pretty), but you'll have to face it eventually, and dog hair will make it much worse in the end.

If you're feeling brave, try the wives' tale remedies: sniffing a little mentholated rub; drinking a Prairie Oyster (Worcestershire, lemon juice, a raw egg, and a small splash of vodka); or drinking an Eye Opener (a raw egg and lemon juice in a shot of whiskey or gin).

While only time will clear the toxins out of your system, you can help by drinking water, juice, Gatorade, or Lucozade. Take a multivitamin as well.

Take a hot shower, sauna, or a steambath. Get rid of those puffy bags under your eyes: Take a tablespoon and submerge it in a glass full of ice water for about a minute. Then close your eye and cup the chilled spoon gently over the lid.

If you can resist eating much of anything for a few hours and concentrate on rehydrating, when you do eat it should mark the end of your hangover. And next time, start with Part One: Preventatives.

THE MOROCCAN ODYSSEY

INSPIRED BY GERALD POSNER

The legendary African and Asian spice routes yielded more than a wealth of cinnamon, nutmeg, cardamom, licorice, ginger, pepper, and other exotic treats that made food and drink taste so much better. Many of these botanical wonders were bound for European gin and vermouth distillers who added the precious ingredients to their secret formulations.

The road to Timbuktu also appropriately serves as the backdrop for a fabulous modern-day adventure, recounted for us by author and journalist Gerald Posner:

> Several years ago my wife, Trisha, and I visited Marrakesh, and after a few days decided to venture south over the Atlas Mountains toward the edge of the Sahara desert. After a couple of days of travel, and spending nights in centuries-old kasbahs along the way, we reached the outpost of Zagora. It was there that the paved road ended and the Sahara started in earnest (our journey ended there). At the edge of Zagora is a sign posted in both Arabic and French, announcing "52 DAYS BY CAMEL TO TIMBUKTU."
>
> A few blocks away from that intimidating notice is a café/coffee shop run by a slightly disheveled Bedouin. It was nearly sunset when we made our way into his shop, empty except for a couple of Arab men in the corner sipping mint tea. My wife and I needed a pick-me-up.
>
> "Coffee?" No.
>
> "Cold water." No.

Shake

2 oz. (60 ml) Beefeater gin

0.5 oz. (15 ml) dry sherry

1 pinch ground cinnamon

If you can find it, try Paarl Oloroso: a dry sherry imported from South Africa.

Here are a few appropriate toasts if you're traveling to Africa or the Middle East:

- Egypt: *Fee sihetak!*
- Tanzania: *Kwa afya yako!*
- Israel: *L'Chayim!*

The Goldfinger served at Lola's at Century House blends 2 oz. (60 ml) Stolichnaya Gold vodka and 1 splash Goldschläger. If you're feeling rich, crumple a sheet of gold leaf into the glass for the garnish.

Lola's at Century House **Gotham** mixed 2 oz. (60 ml) Stolichnaya vodka and 1 splash Luxardo Sambuca Passione Nera.

SPICE LIQUEURS AND CORDIALS

ANISE/LICORICE:
Luxardo Sambuca Passione Nera, absinthe, Pernod, Ouzo

CARAWAY:
kümmel

CINNAMON:
Goldschläger

COFFEE:
Kahlúa, Tia Maria

GINGER:
Domaine de Canton Ginger Liqueur

HERBS, AND SPICES:
Bénedictine, Chartreuse, Yellow Chartreuse, Jägermeister, Galliano, Tuaca, Strega

NUTS:
amaretto (almond), Frangelico (hazelnut), Nocello (walnut)

PEPPERMINT:
peppermint schnapps, crème de menthe

We declined the owner's offer of mint tea, having had enough in the last week to last a lifetime. "Lemonade," my wife took a wild stab. Just a grunt and shake of the head.

We were ready to leave when Trisha almost mumbled to me, "What I would really like is an icy Martini."

"Martini?" It was as though the Bedouin had suddenly received a slight electrical jolt. He popped up from behind his wooden counter, reached into a corner behind a sink, and to our astonishment proudly displayed a classic Martini glass. A big smile crossed his face at our puzzlement.

We looked at each other and almost simultaneously moved back to grab two chairs at a table. The whole purpose of this journey was adventure, so how could we be foolish enough to walk away from this. To this day, we are not quite sure what ingredients our "bartender" mixed, but it was definitely a heavy dose of gin (that, judging by its roughness, must have been aging in the Saharan sun for some time) and I thought there was some white wine added, although Trisha tasted sherry (she's British, so may have a natural inclination to sherry that should probably be discounted!). An olive, stuffed with an anchovy, was plopped into each glass (don't try that one yourself). Everything was served at room temperature, but considering the alternative of mint tea, it was a particularly wonderful Martini. It was far from the best Martini we have ever had, but we don't remember one that was timed better or more appreciated. One though was definitely enough, as we figured it was after three or four of these that tourists inevitably decided the fifty-two days by camel to Timbuktu sounded reasonable.

COPENHAGEN

ADAPTED FROM A RECIPE BY KINGSLEY AMIS

An old friend from Denmark came for a visit recently. When we offered him a cocktail, he said, "In my country we always drink until the liquor cabinet's empty." We'd just bought a couple bottles of vodka and a bottle of akvavit (aka: aquavit), and let him open the cabinet figuring he'd be eating those words when he saw the amount of booze in it. He pulled open the cupboard, stepped back . . . and grinned. We knew it was going to be a long night.

As he began shaking the first round of double-strength, high-potency Copenhagens, we realized our fears were well founded. In a last-ditch effort to avert excruciating hangovers (and to give us a snowball's chance of clearing out the whole cabinet), we invited everyone we could get on the phone. Unfortunately, every time we got someone on the line, he'd shout out in the background, "Tell 'em to bring more booze." Good thing we'd stocked up on almonds before he arrived.

Shake

2 oz. (60 ml)
Smirnoff vodka

0.5 oz. (15 ml)
akvavit

blanched almonds

Kingsley Amis believed the almond was placed in this drink as a Nordic good-luck token and wrote it "will keep your guests' tongues wagging until the liquor sets them wagging about anything under the sun."

For those of you who've never encountered "Scandinavian courage" (aka: akvavit), it's a clear liquid that looks, pours, and is served like a another Nordic favorite—vodka. However, Akvavit's taste has a lot more in common with a loaf of rye bread than with winter wheat. That's right, it's distilled with caraway seeds just like its liqueur cousin—kümmel.

Actress Rosalind Russell's father-in-law, Carl Brisson, introduced her to an Akvavit Martini, shaking 2 oz. (60 ml) akvavit, 0.5 oz. (15 ml) dry vermouth, and 1 dash Angostura bitters. We now know it as the **Rosalind Russell Martini.**

BLACK TEA MARTINI

CREATED BY HIDETSUGU UENO AT BAR HIGH FIVE, TOKYO

Stir

1.5 oz. (45 ml) English-tea-infused vodka

1 tsp. tea liqueur

Rinse the ice in the mixing glass with 4 atomizer sprays of Martini Bianco vermouth.

I was going to make a "tea version of Black Russian" but I found out it works for the Martini style, so . . .

—Hidetsugu Ueno

ESSENTIAL JAPANESE PHRASES:

Sumi ma sen. Martini, o kudasai. (Excuse me. A Matini, please.)

Oribu o irette kudasai. (Please put in an olive.)

Lemon no kawa o irette kudasai. (Please put in a lemon skin.)

There's more to Tokyo nightlife than eating your fill of sushi, yakitori, or sukiyaki and catching a Kabuki theater performance. Our friend Hideo took us out on the town, despite our severe case of jet lag. The twelve-hour time difference was only a minute portion of what turned out to be an eye-opening experience. After dining at a Roppongi country-style restaurant on fresh sea bass, grilled prawns, and Asahi beer, we proceeded to the first cocktail bar, where we found out our guide's nickname was Scotch Up.

Somehow we found ourselves in a karaoke bar after a few rounds, with Scotch Up asking which bottles to buy for us. Within minutes we were dubbed Martini and Extra Dry, and a pair of bottles was added to the shelf in front of us with our names on them. It's much cheaper in Japanese bars to buy a whole bottle, and have them hold on to it for you, unless the people you're drinking with think it's high time everybody finished their bottles. *Kan-pai!*

We were all set for a good night's sleep by four in the afternoon and finally in bed by midnight. At 4 a.m. we were both wide awake and inexplicably starving. Luckily, the Tokyo Fish Market is open at that hour, as the fishing boats roll in round the clock, and the finest of the catch is served up right there—as raw and fresh as it was in the water.

Too bad that when we went to Tokyo our favorite rockabilly bartender Hidetsugu Ueno had not opened his Bar High Five, a pocket-size, hidden gem overlooking the Ginza from its fourth-floor vantage point.

It isn't just the way that he hand-carves his ice for presentation in drinks. Neither is it the mastery he has over stirring and shaking and, okay, doing everything a classic bartender does. Except Ueno does it with remarkable style and understatement.

There's a lot of huzzah in the cocktail world about Japanese bartending techniques. But when you ask Ueno what he thinks makes Japanese bartending so special, he shrugs and says, "Nothing!"

On this point, we don't agree, Ueno-san.

The **Japanese Martini** shakes 2 oz. (60 ml) Suntory Juhyo Shochu and 1 splash Suntory Zen Green Tea Liqueur, garnished with a fresh mint leaf.

Back in 2006, Anistatia came up with **The Anastasia**, which shakes 2 oz. (60 ml) Heavy Water vodka, 2 oz. (60 ml) fresh pink grapefruit juice, 0.25 oz. (10 ml) spiced tea syrup, 0.5 egg white, and 2 dashes of Regan's Orange Bitters. (See the spiced tea syrup recipe on page 197.)

The distinctive aroma of bergamot orange peel in Earl Grey tea inspired Audrey Saunders of Pegu Club to make her famed **Earl Grey MarTEAni** by shaking 0.75 oz. (25 ml) fresh lemon juice, 1 oz. (30 ml) 1:1 simple syrup, 1.5 oz. Earl Grey tea-infused Tanqueray gin, and 1 egg white, garnished with a lemon twist. (See the Earl Grey tea-infused gin recipe on page 195.)

Jared was inspired by the delicate fragrance of Lady Grey tea with its blend of black tea, bergamot, Seville oranges, lemon peel, orange peel, and cornflower petals to blatantly hijack Audrey's original and create a **Lady Grey Martini** that shakes 1.5 oz. (45 ml) Sipsmith London Dry Gin, infused with Lady Grey tea, 0.75 oz. (20 ml) fresh lemon juice, 0.75 oz. (20 ml) simple syrup, and 1 egg white. (See the Lady Grey tea-infused gin recipe on page 195.)

BOHEMIAN MARTINI

CREATED BY TOMAS CAMBRAL AT PAPARAZZI, BRATISLAVA

Stir

1.5 oz. (45 ml) Slovácká Borovička

1.5 oz. (45 ml) Gancia dry vermouth

2 dashes Becherovka

2 dashes Becherovka Cordial

lemon twist

It's amazing how the globalization of the modern Martini has inspired regional creations that will blow your socks off. That sentiment has happened to us in the most seemingly unlikely places: Athens, Perpignan, Barcelona, Moscow, and most recently Bratislava, a capital city nestled between the capital cities of Vienna and Budapest.

We knew of Paparazzi a few years earlier, when we first met our friend Stanislav Vadrna, who was head bartender there before he took on the mantle of most knowledgable western bartender in the art of applying Japanese bartending techniques. (That's another story.)

It was the 2011 Slovak Bar Awards and we were judging three of the finest young talents you could ever imagine. It was Tomas Cambral's turn at the mahogany. This head bartender at Paparazzi knew us well enough by reputation that he conjectured we might ask him to make us a Martini. He was right. What he stirred up was a blend of Slovakian specialities: a juniper spirit called Slovácká Borovička with dashes of Becherovka Cordial (a white wine liqueur infused with linden flowers), and Becherovka, which can be described only as a taste of Christmas—a profusion of warm spices.

Although the other competitors were equally brilliant, Tomas proved to us that the equation of basic Martini recipe plus spiced-predominant regional specialties plus passion plus talent equals a fabulous drink!

We reflected on how many of those wonderfully warm spices that remind most of us of Christmas are found in drinks these days: cinnamon, ginger, nutmeg, cardamom, allspice. All of them achieve the sort of complexity that harkens back to the precocktail era, when Elizabethan, Georgian, and Victorian tavern keepers made up barrels of Hypocras, Bishop, Mulled Wine, Mulled Cider, Cups, and Flasks to warm the cockles and hearts of their patrons on bone-chilling nights. With advancements in insulation and heating, we can only appreciate these aromas and characters for what they are—yummy.

The Raincity Grill in Seattle served a **Spicy Rose Martini**, shaking 2 oz. (60 ml) cardamom-infused vodka and 1 splash rose water.

Dick Bradsell created the **Ivan the Terrible Cocktail**, shaking 2 oz. (60 ml) Ivan the Terrible Vodka and splashes of honey water and fresh lemon juice, garnished with a dusting of ground cinnamon. (See the honey water recipe on page 197.)

Dré Masso created a **Mulled Wine Martini** for Santa's in London, shaking 0.75 oz. (25 ml) Beefeater gin, 0.75 oz. (25 ml) port, the juice of half an orange (chopped and muddled), 0.5 oz. (15ml) lemon juice, 0.25 oz. (10 ml) honey water, 2 crushed cloves, 1 pinch cinnamon powder, and 1 sprinkle grated nutmeg, garnished with a clove-studded orange. (See the honey water recipe on page 197.)

Richard Hunt at the Hawksmoor at Seven Dials makes a **Pickle Finger Martini**, shaking 0.75 oz. (20 ml) clementine syrup, 0.75 oz. (20 ml) lemon juice, 1.5 oz. (45 ml) Oxley gin, 1 splash Stone's Ginger Wine, 1 egg white, and 1 dash orange bitters. (See the clementine syrup recipe on page 198.)

For a unique drinking and dining experience, try Bratislava's UFO restaurant. Picture a UFO perched atop one of the towers on San Francisco's Golden Gate Bridge and you get a pretty good image of this high point of Communist-era construction hovering high over the Danube. The panorama is unparalleled, as is the feeling when a heavy truck crosses the bridge. The whole place hits about 4.0 on the Richter scale. Add to that a diagonal elevator ride up and down inside one of the bridge abutments, plus first-rate bartenders at the top, and it becomes truly unforgettable, in a good way. Was it a truck or that last Martini?

COCONUT MARTINI

CREATED BY DUSHAN ZARIC AT PRAVDA, NEW YORK

Shake

2 oz. (60 ml) coconut vodka

1 oz. (30 ml) pineapple purée

0.5 oz. (15 m) simple syrup

0.5 oz. (15 ml) lime juice

coconut flakes

(For the coconut vodka recipe, see page 195.)

When we first walked downstairs into Pravda in New York back in the 1990s, we couldn't help notice that something wonderful was going on behind the bar. Jason Kosmas and Dushan Zaric weren't just offering up beautiful shots of vodka and cold-as-ice Vodka Martinis, they were having fun playing with all sorts of vodka infusions, an Eastern European tradition that unearthed itself from the realm of Russian and Polish restaurants into the world of hip drinking parlors in both the United States and Britain.

A remarkable take on our favorite poolside sip, the Piña Colada, Dushan had divined a Coconut Martini that checked every box even without the pool, swimwear, sunglasses, fluorescent cocktail cherries, and ubiquitous pastel-hued cocktail umbrella.

It was a humid, hotter-than-a-convection oven evening in Greenwich Village when we encountered this drink. The frosty concoction was on its second round. Just enough to fortify our trek up Lafayette Street to dig into a round of sushi.

Talking about the tropical side of life reminds us of a story someone sent us about a harrowing Martini adventure:

> While vacationing in Hawaii and staying at the Four Seasons, my husband had a Martini experience. He got out of the shower one morning and noticed a red dime-size spot on his wrist. I proceeded to tell him that a woman had gotten bitten by a brown spider while vacuuming, lapsed into a coma, and, by the time they found her they had to cut off both her arms and her legs! This didn't cheer him up. We stopped at

the concierge to show him . . . and he let us know that in Hawaii they take bites very seriously.

Despite that we went out and had a late night full of Martinis. We stopped at the lobby bar for a "final final" one and met a couple on their honeymoon. We showed the bartender the bite, and the couple had also heard the story about the woman and the brown spider. They offered to buy John his "final" drink. We all had a good laugh.

We went to bed (or maybe passed out), but around 12:30 a.m. I was awakened by a knock at the door . . . I ignored it, because who did I know in Maui? The knocking came again. I knew that my husband . . . way on the other side of the king-size bed . . . would never hear it, so I got up.

I first peered through the keyhole, then opened the door and found my husband stark naked in the hallway. My first response was, "Where have you been?" He was not amused. He seemed to have walked in his sleep . . . which he had never done before . . . and awoke just in time to watch the door lock shut!! Now he was naked in the hallway of a five-star hotel!! Luckily, I woke up and let him in. It has been great fun over and over in the retelling!!!

Was it the bite or the Martinis? We'll probably never know!

The Spider Bite shakes 2 oz. (60 ml) Moskovskaya vodka, 0.5 oz. (15 ml) Malibu coconut rum, 0.5 oz. (15 ml) triple sec, and 2 drops Angostura bitters, garnished with a lime twist.

What's worse after a pleasant evening—including one too many Martinis—than going to brush your teeth and seeing a gigantic spider on the bathroom wall? Regaining composure, returning to the bathroom, and not being able to locate the hairy beast again. Next time we visit Aunt Bobbie, we'll try not to show up in the midst of the tarantula migration again.

Tropical twists can sometimes spell the
end of a serious cocktail. (Just try to look
sophisticated while clutching a big frosty
Piña Colada.) You'll be happy to know that
among the hundreds of Modern Martini
recipes we've encountered, we haven't
uncovered a single one that was garnished
with a cocktail umbrella. A small plastic
hula girl, yes. But not a paper umbrella.

But maybe that little parasol is just the
thing for the Extra-Dry
Martini lover. It would
ward off excess humid-
ity and protect the drink
from dilution during a
sudden thunderstorm.

CAJUN MARTINI

AS SERVED AT BOMBAY CLUB, NEW ORLEANS

Singer Jimmy Buffet croons about a Cajun Martini in his song, "We Are the People Our Parents Warned Us About." But where did this little slice of liquid fire come from? Renowned Louisiana chef Paul Prudhomme is often cited as the inventor of the Cajun Martini—although by his own admission, it was unintentional. As he stated in a recent interview (to be read as it was spoken, with a thick Louisiana accent):

> We actually started it as a joke because we didn't want to serve hard liquor and we had a license and we wanted to maintain the license as part of the agreement with the landlord . . . so . . . we put a cayenne pepper and a jalapeño pepper into a bottle of vodka and a bottle of gin and put a little vermouth in the serving. And I think the first one[s] lasted about three months. Then all of a sudden . . . we were selling two or three gallons a night.

Fortunately the genius of this creation wasn't lost on its creator, and Prudhomme quickly came out with his own line of ready-to-pour bottles of Cajun Martinis.

What is all this Cajun stuff? Sometimes we forget that the rest of the world doesn't have Louisiana in its living room and Mexico right next door. So for those of you who don't immediately see what's so funny about Chevy marketing their Nova model south of the border (in Spanish *no va* translates to "it doesn't go"), a jalapeño is a little green chile that might be considered more appropriate for use in massage balm. But we love nibbling them

Shake

1 oz. (30 ml) pepper-infused vodka

1 oz. (30 ml) Absolut Citron

0.25 oz. (10 ml) dry vermouth

2 Tabasco-spiced olives

To make Tabasco-spiced olives, drain the brine from a jar of green olives. Add 2 tablespoons Tabasco sauce. Cover tightly and shake to coat the olives. Marinate in the refrigerator for at least 1 hour.

"I only drink Martinis to cure what ails me."

"Why, what ails you?"

"Absolutely nothing. That's how well they work!"

Although everyone has memories they'd love to relive, sometimes it's the moments we'd never want to repeat that are the most memorable. We were sitting in Nave's Bar on a sunny afternoon in Fairfax, California, when "shaken" took on a whole new meaning. Steve the bartender had just loaded up a shaker and put the lid on it when a tremor hit. We'll never know if he was paralyzed with fright or the coolest bartender in the world at that moment, but with the room rolling and the bottles rattling, he just stood there motionless for half a minute holding the lid on the shaker. When it was over, he didn't say a word—or give the drink a single extra shake. He simply strained the contents into a waiting glass, slid it across the bar to the person who'd ordered it (and finally emerged from under a table to claim it), and wiped down the bar. Needless to say, we ordered our next round stirred.

to remind ourselves (through the ensuing agony) just how wonderful life really is. Cajun cooking—though it traces some of its roots back to France—is truly unique to the bayous of the Deep South.

If you're still wincing at the challenge of drinking chile-laced spirits, think about the fact that they're certainly an improvement over the 1930s version of a peppery Martini. The Miner's Cocktail consisted of two jiggers of gin, a splash of lemon juice, and two hefty pinches of fresh-ground black pepper.

Jeffrey Smith's **Cajun Martini**, which has also been dubbed The Inferno, blends 1 jigger Stolichnaya Pertsovka, 1 splash olive juice, and a stuffed green olive garnish.

The Peppertini at Oliver's at the Mayflower Park Hotel blends 2 oz. (60 ml) Absolut Pepper vodka over ice rinsed with 1 splash Cinzano dry vermouth. Red and black pepper flakes are sprinkled on top and a marinated olive is added as garnish.

Sean Hamilton's **Spicy Hamilton** gets its kick from Tabasco sauce, mixing 2 oz. (60 ml) Skyy vodka, 1 oz. (30 ml) Cinzano dry vermouth, and 3 drops Tabasco. Rim the glass with lime and top the mix with a lemon twist.

The **Mansion Martini** served at the Rosewood Mansion on Turtle Creek in Dallas uses a tequila rinse for the ice, shakes up 3 oz. (90 ml) Bombay Sapphire Gin, and garnishes it with a jalapeño pepper-filled olive.

Lola's at Century House served a **Pepper Spray**, shaking 3 oz. (90 ml) vodka infused with tri-colored peppercorns. (See tri-colored peppercorn infused vodka recipe on page 196.)

The 1930s **Miner's Cocktail** stirred 3 oz. (90 ml) gin, 1 splash lemon juice, and 2 large pinches of ground black pepper.

TRUFFLE MARTINI

CREATED BY BY JARED BROWN AT SIPSMITH DISTILLERY, LONDON

You can call them the culinary version of "black gold." The world knows them as black truffles. No. We're not talking about the chocolate morsels that appear every Christmas in gourmet chocolate shops. We're talking about the aromatic fungus that sends the French, Spanish, and Italians to the forests to root around the bases of oak and hazel trees. These gnarly lumps are transformed in the kitchen, slice by tender slice, as a topping on beef filets with foie gras, a garnish on risotto, an absolutely scandalous truffled macaroni and cheese. There's a reason for the paltry servings, aside from the rich flavor. Black truffles cost around $2,000 per pound!

So when Jared asked Chef Giorgio Locatelli for one of his precious morsels at the height of his seasonal all-truffle menu, you can imagine the lecture he got about how carefully to tend it until he cautiously sliced it with a mandolin. Giorgio had a reason to be apprehensive. Jared explained that he was going to infuse his gin with this piece of "black gold" to make a Truffle Martini for a pop-up restaurant at the Sipsmith Distillery. (Jared had come upon the idea after tasting the vermouth infused with white truffles that 69 Colebrooke Row's Tony Conigliaro cooked up.)

When the pop-up's reservation list increased threefold, Jared went back to Giorgio to purchase another truffle. Giorgio was not keen on another truffle swimming in vodka. Luckily Jared brought a sample of his precious infusion. After he had a taste, Girogio handed him his second-to-last truffle with a warm, paternal smile.

Stir

2 oz. (60 ml) truffle-infused Sipsmith Barley vodka

1 oz. (30ml) Noilly Prat dry vermouth

slice of black truffle

(See the recipe for truffle-infused vodka on page 195.)

Albert Trummer, when he presided at New York's Town Restaurant, made a **Town Truffle Martini** that shook 3.5 oz. Hennessy XO cognac, 1 splash fresh lime juice, 1 splash 100-year-old Grand Marnier, and 2 thin slices of black truffle, garnished with 5 slices of black truffle.

TUSCAN MARTINI

CREATED BY KATHY CASEY FOR FRANKIE'S ITALIAN RESTAURANT, ABU DHABI

Shake

3 oz. (90 ml)
Luksusowa vodka or Beefeater gin

1 tsp. grappa-and-lemon-infused dry
vermouth

lemon, rosemary, and garlic
marinated olives

(See the recipes for
grappa-and-lemon-infused
dry vermouth and lemon,
rosemary, and garlic
marinated olives on pages
196 and 198.)

There's a wonderful custom in Italy. It's called aperitivo. Yes, that's Italian for appetizer, but in Italy it's more than that. It's a ritual. We encountered it in Turin, Verona, and even in little villages in Chianti. At cocktail hour, you peruse the cocktail list, but if you're smart and adventurous, order the house aperitif. Almost invariably, when the drinks arrive, yours will come with a little side dish even if no one else's does. That's because you've shown your faith in the place, and that should be rewarded. At Caffé Mulasanno it was pizettas on a small cake stand (by the way, if you visit Turin, aside from making a trip to see where Martini & Rossi comes from, you have to get a bottle of Mulasanno's Liquori di Alpi, a house aperitif wine made just for them for a century or so). At another café it was an assortment of finger sandwiches. At another we were directed to help ourselves from the sideboard. Food completes the sensory experience of drink, especially when you're drinking aperitivi, which our friend Giuseppe Gallo likes to point out means to prepare the stomach for food. Food presented as an assortment of little bites, like the aperitivi or tapas, is that much more romantic as it is made for sharing. And what are shared experiences if not romantic encounters?

WAKE-UP CALL

CREATED BY JARED BROWN

The Wake-Up Call was our first major attempt at infusing vodka with fresh spices. We'd sampled some interesting combinations at our local Russian restaurant, Russian Samovar in Midtown Manhattan (where gallon-size glass jars of fruit-infused, vegetable-infused, and spice-infused vodkas proudly stood behind the bar), but it wasn't until a blizzard shut down the entire city for a few days that we tried our hand at it. (After all, the bars and grocery stores were shut tighter than a drum, leaving us to our own devices and the contents of our refrigerator.)

The result was exactly what the doctor ordered: The blood-warming spiciness was a welcome tonic during the frozen days that followed. In fact, it was so effective, we built three snowmen in subfreezing temperatures without getting frostbitten.

Shake

2 oz. (60 ml)
vodka infused with fresh ginger slices
and lemon twists

lemon twist

(See ginger-and-lemon-infused
vodka recipe on page 193.)

The Wild Ginger made at the Wild Ginger restaurant in Seattle pours 3 oz. (90 ml) vodka infused with fresh ginger with a lemon twist garnish as their signature Martini.

The Olympic Gold at the Garden Court in the Fairmont Olympic blends 1 oz. (30 ml) each of both Bombay Sapphire Gin and Absolut Citron, splashes of Domaine de Canton Ginger Liqueur and Martell Cordon Bleu cognac.

PINEAPPLE & CARDAMOM MARTINI

CREATED BY HENRY BESANT FOR THE LONSDALE, LONDON

Shake

2 oz. (60 ml)
Ketel One vodka

2 oz. (60 ml)
pressed fresh pineapple juice

1 splash sugar syrup

4 whole green cardamom pods

Long after London's famous Criterion Restaurant, site of endless cocktail-fueled celebrations in the 1920s, had vanished, the space was a Boots pharmacy. When they decided to move across the street a demolition crew entered the building but stopped before the first hammer was swung. There above the drop ceiling and behind the wall panels lay the bejeweled Art Deco interior of the original Criterion, with its Egyptian accents. And there it stands today on Piccadilly Circus, still serving great drinks to thirsty Americans (and Brits, too).

Green cardamom triggers memories of the topping on New York crumb cake, fresh from the oven at Zabar's on the Upper West Side. It reminds us of endless take-aways at the local Indian restaurant, which we love. There's something about this insidious little spice, the world's most expensive by weight, that makes us crave curries, chai, pilaus, and biryanis as well. Coupled with pineapple it gives sage a run for its money. Although we have to admit we first encountered the marriage of pineapple and sage in Nick Strangeway's Sage Pineapple Mojito and Sage Pineapple Margarita before we knew that the pairing of pineapple and cardamom existed.

Let's face it. The marriage of pineapple with a number of so-called savory spices is a union made in heaven.

Nick Strangeway's **Pineapple Sage Mojito** builds 8 young sage leaves, 0.5 oz. (15 ml) pineapple purée, 0.75 oz. (20 ml) fresh lime juice, 1 tsp. sugar syrup, and 1.5 oz. Havana Club Añejo Blanco rum.

THE BOTTOM LINE
ON SPECIALTY MARTINIS

Creating a classic Martini is about being creative within a tight set of rules. Dreaming up a new specialty Martini is still about following a set of rules, albeit a much broader set. Not every creation that lands in a V-bowled stemmed glass should be declared a Martini. Certainly not a drink using citrus instead of vermouth as a modifier, or otherwise more closely resembling and evolved from a different category of classic. And that, in short, is the crucible of cocktail creation—knowing the classics intimately enough to draw on them when you branch out. It's like erecting a skyscraper. Unless there's a solid foundation, the rest of it is going nowhere. For specialty Martinis, the first tenet is simplicity, few ingredients. The next is balance. Strength needs to be balanced by dilution. Many young professional mixers today taste each new creation by dipping a straw into it. This does not replicate the experience of actually drinking that drink. It is essential to try a whole drink when you're experimenting, which is why it can take some time to create a new one. Audrey Saunders tests each drink on her cocktail list at least a hundred times before it makes it onto the list.

We were styling drinks for the launch of a new gin. After the photo shoot, we asked if we could take a couple bottles for a friend. They said yes, but asked us not to share them with anyone in the media. We kept our promise, but took them straight to Pegu Club, along with photographer Shin Ohira and his crew (all off-duty and without cameras). They were all Japanese and hadn't been to Pegu, or many other New York bars. I handed Audrey the gin bottles and we ordered drinks for the five of us. Shortly after our drinks arrived, Audrey appeared with a tray of thirty-odd variations on the Gimlet. She offloaded them onto the table, pointing out ones she found better or worse than the others. Our guests were gobsmacked. "Which do I drink?" asked one of the assistants, who'd lost his cocktail in the sea on the table. Audrey gave a beneficent "help yourself" wave and disappeared. "Are American bars all like this?" he asked, eyeing the five drinks to each person on the table. Anistatia laughed, "Of course they are."

PASSIONATE ELIXIRS

MARTINIS BUILT FOR TWO

Hovering near the top of the Top Ten Things That Two Can Do Better Than One is having a Martini. If you haven't gotten the hint yet, Martinis have sex appeal. What other drink inspires discussions about smooth fire, Fred Astaire dance steps, cool jazz, and candlelit surroundings? Martinis spell sophisticated, seductive romance, especially when you make them for two.

A romantic tête-à-tête isn't difficult to arrange. All you need is a dose of Hollywood inspiration: Set the stage, check your props (the bar is set up and stocked, glasses are sparkling clean, the food is ready, the flowers are in position), make sure your costume fits, call makeup if you must, brush up on your mixology, and rehearse your sexiest lines. Don't forget to remove any roommates, drop kids off at Grandma's house, turn the phone or Skype off, and switch the background music on. And make sure that the one you love is in the mood.

We've found a few memorable scenarios and recipes made with the finest ingredients to ignite your imagination. But we're sure you have a couple of your own, too.

A shy English major was astonished when the school's best-looking cheerleader accepted his invitation to go out for Martinis.

By the third drink he'd completely run out of small talk. In desperation he asked, "Do you like Kipling?"

To his surprise, her eyes lit up, and she smiled for the first time all night, but she didn't answer.

He leaned closer and asked again, "Do you?"

"Well, I don't know," she replied between giggles, "I've never kippled."

FLAME OF LOVE, REVISITED

CREATED BY AUDREY SAUNDERS

Stir

2.5 oz. (75 ml) bay leaf-infused Absolut

0.75 oz. (20 ml) apple-infused Lustau Fino Sherry

1 dash house orange bitters

4 orange twists

flaming orange twist

Flame 4 orange twists into a cocktail glass. Discard twists. Add ice into a mixing glass, then pour in vodka and sherry. Stir and strain into the prepared glass. Flame an orange twist over the top.

(See pages 194 and 196 for bay leaf-infused vodka and apple-infused sherry.)

Audrey's **Bay Leaf Martini** stirs 1.5 oz. (45 ml) bay leaf-infused Absolut, 0.75 oz. (20 ml) Tio Pepe Fino Sherry, and 0.75 oz. (20 ml) Dolin dry vermouth, garnished with a fresh bay leaf.

When the flames of love are fanned more than once, it leads to something more intense—passion. Smoldering in every great relationship is a desire to rekindle that first encounter, that first embrace, that first kiss.

If you're inclined to believe that love carries sensations of excitement and mystery, then you'll understand that romance doesn't end when you've tied the knot, spent years living the day to day with the same person. It can be a quiet evening, holding hands while watching a DVD. It can be a quiet stroll through the park or sharing an ice cream cone. Better yet, surprising the one you love with a candlelit dinner for two, apéritifs for two, and the kids safely tucked away at the grandparents' for the night.

Why are we waxing philosophic about the flames of love? Because it reminds us of a Martini that Pepe Ruiz, bartender at Chasen's in Hollywood, created for Dean Martin. The flaming twist he used as a garnish never ceases to spark excitement and anticipation. No matter how many times you see it done.

Pepe Ruiz's **Flames of Love** rinses a chilled cocktail glass with 3 drops of La Ina sherry. Squeeze an orange twist over the glass and then flame the twist over the glass. Throw away the peel. Add ice to chill again. Throw the ice out. Add 2 oz. (60 ml) vodka. Flame another orange twist around the rim and throw it out.

SHAKEN NOT STIRRED

LA DOLCE VITA

CREATED BY HOLGER FAULHAMMER

Maybe you're feeling lyrical. A candlelit Italian dinner for two has melted many romantic hearts, so there must be something to it. You can start off by sharing a round of rosy-hued La Dolce Vitas while you nibble at a Caprese of fresh tomatoes and buffalo mozzarella garnished with fresh basil leaves. For the main course, forget the pizza, go for pasta and a salad (unless your culinary imagination and budget sends you in the direction of a slow-cooked osso bucco or a black truffle risotto).

To set the mood, play a sexy opera like Puccini's *Turandot* or *Madama Butterfly* (or you can opt for Malcolm McLaren's "Madame Butterfly"). If it worked for the world's great Italian lovers—Marcello Mastroianni, Rudolph Valentino, Giancarlo Giannini—who knows what the evening will have in store?

A rustic Tuscan picnic is another ideal Italian-style setting that's shown great promise. A picnic basket filled with fruit, fresh bread, cheeses, sausages, and a portable bar is all you need to make a day in the country a special occasion.

Shake

2 oz. (60 ml) Beefeater gin

1 oz. (30 ml) Martini & Rossi extra-dry vermouth

1 oz. (30 ml) Pinot Grigio wine

1 dash Campari

The classic **Negroni** builds 1 oz. (30 ml) Beefeater gin, 1 oz. (30 ml) Martini & Rossi Rosso vermouth, and 1 oz. (30 ml) Campari in a rocks glass filled with ice, garnished with an orange twist.

The Garden Court's **Copper Illusion** shakes 4 oz. (120 ml) Beefeater gin and 0.5 oz. (15 ml) each of Cointreau and Campari.

Oliver's **Sterling Gold** shakes 3 oz. (90 ml) Tanqueray Sterling vodka and 0.5 oz. (15 ml) Tuaca Liqueur.

YIN & YANG MARTINIS

CREATED BY DALE DEGROFF, NEW YORK

Stir

For the Yin Martini:

3 oz. (90 ml)
Ginga Shizuku Junmai Daiginjo sake

0.5 oz. (15 ml) dry gin

fresh lichee or other oriental fruit

For the Yang Martini:

3 oz. (90 ml) dry gin

0.5 oz. (15 ml)
Ginga Shizuku Junmai Daiginjo Sake

olives

If you're heading for Asia, here are a few toasts:

Bali & Indonesia: *Selamat!*
China: *Yam sing!*
(Cantonese)
Taiwan: *Gun Bi!*
India: *Aap ki shubh kai liyai!*; Pakistan: *Jama Sihap!*
Japan: *Kan pai!*
Korea: *Deupstita!*
Thailand: *Chai yo!*

The light and the dark. The warm and the cold. Male and female. Those are the images that truly apply to the Asian concept of yin and yang. They say that opposites not only attract but complete each other. And when it comes to love, yin and yang is the essence, the core of all relationships. The interaction of complementary opposites in temperament, biological makeup, and preferences are what make a relationship a dynamic, thriving entity of its own. Bottom line: Balance is the key to every great pairing. Whether it pertains to love or cocktails. Without balance, you have nothing.

Kathy Casey created a **Zen Garden**, muddling 2-inch-long pieces of celery, 2-inch-long pieces of split lemon grass, and 3 slices fresh cucumber in a mixing glass. Then shaking the contents with 1.5 oz. (45 ml) Hendrick's gin, 0.5 oz. (15 ml) Monin Organic Agave Syrup, 0.75 oz. (20 ml) yuzu juice, and 0.5 oz. (15 ml) sake, garnished with a thin slice of cucumber speared onto a piece of lemon grass.

A sleek and simple **Saketini** shakes 2 oz. (60 ml) Suntory Juhyo Shochu and 1 oz. (30 ml) Gekkeikan Sake, garnished with a lemon twist.

FRENCH KISS

CREATED BY OLIVER'S AT THE MAYFLOWER PARK HOTEL, SEATTLE

Few destinations are as romantic as France. From the cafés and bistros of Paris (we include Harry's New York Bar on this list, of course) to the little villages in Burgundy, to the Mediterranean beaches where *tout la France* gathers each August *en vacance*. A Martini has that same cool sensuality. But can you imagine the effect when a splash of champagne is added to that glass of liquid satin? Now that's a French Kiss. Is this wrong? Of course not. Vermouth is a wine. Champagne is a wine. Both work in a Martini.

Surround that pale, effervescent specter with a table for two dressed in white linen with a single burning white candle and a single long-stemmed red rose. Serve a sensuous dessert like a dish of fresh strawberries kissed with a dollop of fresh whipped cream. (The two of you can reenact Nastassja Kinski's luscious strawberry scene from *Tess*, or just whisper sweet nothings in each other's ear.)

The tempestuous tango may have been invented in Buenos Aires, but its coolly detached sensuality reminds us of dimly lit Parisian bistros. (We're not discussing the *Last Tango in Paris* here.) We're talking about putting on a steamy Astor Piazzolla tango or a sultry Django Reinhardt gypsy jazz ballad, and doing a body-to-body, barefoot tango. Study Jean Gabin's role as Pépé le Moko in the 1937 movie by the same name or Charles Boyer also playing Pépé le Moko in the 1938 American film *Algiers*. (Unlike his cartoon skunk counterpart, Pepe Le Pew, the sexy le Moko always got his woman.) Boyer's discrete yet steamy charm swept

Shake

0.5 oz. (15 ml)
Lillet Blanc

1.5 oz. (45 ml)
Stolichnaya vodka

1 oz. (30 ml)
Moët & Chandon Brut Impérial
champagne

orange twist

Rinse the shaker with Lillet. Add ice and vodka. Shake until cold. Strain and garnish. Add champagne just before serving.

Hedy Lamarr off her feet when he invited her to come with him to the Kasbah.

What we've been talking about all along is a love affair. It may last for a moment or a lifetime, who knows? But like any great passion, it should be eloquent and elegant. The memory should last an eternity.

We walked into a little harbor-side bar in the South of France and took seats at the bar, tucked toward the back away from the blistering sun, heat, and throng of well-oiled tourists nursing their afternoon lattes and *citron pressés*. Anistatia nudged me. "That's Old Granddad and Old Forrester." I followed her gaze. There, mixed in with the usual bar stock, were bottles that had to have been there since the fifties or sixties. Vielle Cure, no longer produced, rare cognacs, even rarer American whiskies, old Chartreuse. The bartender quickly made it clear those bottles were not for sale. Not to be put off, Anistatia simply ordered a Martini made with a splash of the Vielle Cure. The bartender nodded and made her one. We did our best to sample every one of these museum pieces, each a taste of history, and all still in good shape stored in the dim light and constant temperature of the back bar.

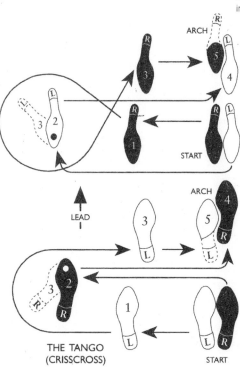

ARCH

LEAD

THE TANGO
(CRISSCROSS)

ARCH

START

START

CHAPTER THREE

IN THE KITCHEN

INFUSED SPIRITS & LUSCIOUS SYRUPS WITH A DASH OF BITTERS

Even while we were writing the first edition of *Shaken Not Stirred®: A Celebration of the Martini,* mixologists were evolving into "liquid chefs," mixologists who, like their pre-Prohibition ancestors, went into the kitchen to make fresh syrups, infused spirits, and other delights to shake, stir, throw, roll, and blend into their creations.

Truth be known, going into the kitchen to make bar ingredients is not a new treat, it's an old and timeless tradition that got lost in the years after Prohibition because there weren't any seasoned veterans to explain to the new pups how to make these noncommercial, personalized ingredients that make a cocktail a work of art.

If you love to play in the kitchen (or you're a chemistry major with a few spare moments), making your own bar ingredients rewards you with the fruits (and spices) of your labors. There are rules. But then, the second you walk into the kitchen as a commis, a sous, a chef, or a mixologist, you realize that the kitchen is a science and that creativity flourished in this hotbed of axioms and equations that can make or break a replicable experiment.

> I am prepared to believe that a dry martini slightly impairs the palate, but think of what it does for the soul.
>
> —Alec Waugh

But you can't call these rules limitations, just the borders in which you've got an entire arena for your wildest ideas. The sky really is the limit. Just most suckers don't know how to raise their arms to reach it.

Here are the first ground rules:

- Always use a clean, sterilized, sealable glass container. Mason jars, clip-up Grolsch-style bottles, and Kilner jars are your best storage units.

- Once your container is cleaned with hot water and soap as well as rinsed in hot water, you can either put it in the dishwasher for a finishing rinse and heated dry or place it in your oven at 350°F/180°C for about twenty minutes to kill any residual bacteria or airborne yeasts that may affect your recipe.

- Despite the numerous recipes on the Web that say you can, never make a spirit infusion with cheap liquor. In the same way that you can't cook a perfect filet mignon with chuck steak, you can't make a batch of drinkable infused spirit that can last you a few years, mellowed with age, if you've used jaw-locking liquor from a plastic bottle.

- Never reuse the same jar without cleaning it according to the above instructions. Bad kitchen habits invite unwanted flavors and chemical reactions.

- Use organically grown ingredients whenever possible. The residual pesticides and fungicides used to protect plants and botanicals during their growth cycle can show up as concentrated, unsavory elements in your creation.

- Never allow your mixture to macerate (the fancy word for infusing ingredients) in a warm place unless it is called for in a specific recipe. You'll change the delicate chemistry that takes place so well in the cool confines of your refrigerator or dark corner of your pantry.

- Never use an infused spirit or fresh-made syrup that's been left unopened in a warm room for days or weeks or months. It's like letting a fine wine go bad by leaving it open on a picnic table. The fruit flies will have a party, but you won't. Throw it out. Things may have grown in that mixture that can hurt you and give mixology a bad name with health and safety.

Practiced carefully, the alchemy of infusion can result in a surprising array of tastes that will impress both avant-Martini sippers and stolid classicists. Who knows, you might go down in *Popular Science*'s Chemists' Hall of Fame with your genius!

To give you a feel for what we're talking about, here are the recipes used by the mixologists who created the drinks in this book.

If you can boil an egg, you can make a Martini. I'm not talking a green-at-the-edges hard-boiled one, though. If you can get an egg to come out creamy in the middle, or if you notice the difference between the two, if you care, you can make a great Martini.

—Jared Brown

INFUSED SPIRITS

GINGER & LEMON VODKA

1 pint (480 ml) high-quality vodka
1 oz. (28 g) fresh, thinly sliced ginger
3 large lemon twists

Transfer the vodka to a canning jar. (Save the bottle.) Add ginger and twists. Seal the container and store it in the fridge overnight. Taste-test the mixture. (If it's too spicy, add more vodka.) Decant the liquid through a gold-mesh coffee filter back into its original bottle and place it in the freezer.

Beech-leaf gin is a great long-lost British recipe. When the beech trees are just unfurling their new leaves, and the leaves are vibrant green and glassy, stuff a jar full of them. Then fill it with enough gin to keep the leaves completely covered. Set it aside for ten to fourteen days in a cupboard or other dark place. At this point, the liquid should have the bright green hue of the leaves. Strain it into a clean bottle. You can keep the color by adding more gin, or keep the intensity of flavor by not adding more and it will turn a beautiful mahogany color. Add sugar to make a traditional British noyau, a hazelnut liqueur. Though it contains no nuts, it does have a very nutty flavor.

JALAPEÑO PEPPER GIN

1 liter dry gin
3 jalapeño peppers, quartered
1 chipotle pepper

Transfer the gin to a canning jar. (Save the bottle.) Add the peppers. Seal the container and store it in the fridge for two weeks. Decant the gin through a gold-mesh coffee filter back into its original bottle and place it in the freezer. If it's too spicy add more gin.

SUN-DRIED CRANBERRY VODKA

1 pint grain vodka
1 cup sun-dried cranberries

Transfer the vodka into a large canning jar. (Save the bottle.) Add the sun-dried cranberries. Seal the container and store it in the fridge overnight. Taste-test the mixture. (If it's too light, leave it in the fridge for one more day.) Decant the liquid through a gold-mesh coffee filter back into its original bottle and throw it in the freezer.

SUN-DRIED CHERRY VODKA

1 pint grain vodka
1 cup sun-dried cherries
3 large orange twists

Transfer the vodka into a large canning jar. (Save the bottle.) Add the sun-dried cherries and orange twists. Seal the container and store it in the fridge overnight. Taste-test the mixture. (If it's too light, leave it in the fridge for one more day.) Decant the liquid through a gold-mesh coffee filter back into its original bottle and throw it in the freezer.

BAY-LEAF VODKA

2 large bay leaves
8 oz. (240ml) vodka

Let steep for 9 hours at room temperature. Strain off and refrigerate.

BASIC COFFEE LIQUEUR

1 cup (240 ml) cooled espresso coffee
½ vanilla bean, split lengthwise
1 cup turbinado sugar
1 cup (480 ml) spirit of choice

Pour the espresso (we prefer Illy Coffee) into a large glass mason jar and add the vanilla bean, sugar, and spirit. Close tightly and steep for 4 weeks. Strain and decant into clean glass bottles.

COCONUT VODKA

1 liter Luksusowa vodka
2 cups dried unsweetened coconut flakes

Infuse ingredients in a clear glass bottle for 3 days and then fine-strain into another clean bottle.

LAVENDER GIN

2 tsp. dried organic lavender
1 liter Plymouth gin

Place lavender in a small saucepan. Add 2 cups (480 ml) Plymouth gin and bring to a boil. Immediately remove from the heat and allow to cool. Add remaining gin. Strain the mixture into a clean bottle. Store at room temperature, away from sunlight.

EARL GREY GIN

4 tbsp. Earl Grey tea
750 ml Tanqueray gin

Measure loose tea into the bottle of gin. Cap and shake, and let sit at room temperature for 2 hours. Strain through a fine sieve or coffee filter into a bowl. Rinse out the bottle to remove the loose tea, and pour the infusion back into the clean bottle.

LADY GREY GIN

4 tbsp. Lady Grey tea
700 ml Sipsmith gin

Measure loose tea into the bottle of gin. Cap and shake, and let sit at room temperature for 2 hours. Strain through a fine sieve or coffee filter into a bowl. Rinse out the bottle to remove the loose tea, and pour the infusion back into the clean bottle.

BLACK TRUFFLE VODKA

2 small black truffles, thinly sliced
700 ml Sipsmith Barley vodka

Infuse truffle slices and vodka in a large mason jar or Kilner jar for 10 days. Strain and store in a tightly closed bottle away from sunlight until ready to use.

Always label your experiments. There's nothing worse than tasting your way through the cupboard searching for the beech-leaf gin and getting a mouthful of wormwood bitters. It happened the other day and no amount of gargling removed it. Breakfast after that simply didn't taste right.

TWIST WITH CARE

I ordered a Martini with a twist. The bartender iced the glass, iced the mixing glass, and reloaded it with fresh ice. He stirred it effortlessly and strained it into the frosty glass. Then he cut a twist with a channel knife, scooping up equal parts peel and pith, wrapped it tightly around a swizzle stick to give it a spiral shape, and deftly knotted it, wringing out every drop of citrus oil before he got it anywhere near the drink. He waved it back and forth with a flourish over the drink as if this would resuscitate the now-dead twist (or pull a rabbit out of the Martini), and dropped it in. It was very pretty, but he couldn't have purged it more completely of any trace of flavor short of stomping on it and running it under the tap.

A bartender swearing allegiance to only one gin today is like a chef insisting that only basil will do, and refusing to cook with oregano or thyme. There are so many flavor differences amongst gins of the highest quality.

I love vermouth. I like to drink it on the rocks, or garnished with dry gin and a twist, or with rye, bitters, and a cherry.

TRI-COLORED PEPPERCORN VODKA

16 tbsp. (160 gr) tri-colored peppercorns
750 ml vodka

Crush peppercorns in a food mill or using a mortar and pestle until the texture is like coarse-ground coffee. Place the peppercorns in a clean mason jar or Kilner jar. Add the vodka. Cover tightly and shake vigorously for about 20 seconds. Place in a cool, dark space and steep for about 3 weeks. Strain through a cheesecloth or muslin jelly bag into a clean glass bottle. Store in a dark space for future use.

GREEN SHISO SHOCHU

12 fresh green shiso leaves
750 ml bottle lichiko shochu

Infuse shiso leaves in shochu in a clean mason jar or Kilner jar for 5 to 7 days. Strain into a clean bottle and refrigerate until ready to use.

INFUSED APERITIFS

APPLE-INFUSED SHERRY

8 Macintosh apples, sliced paper-thin with a mandoline
1 liter Lustau Fino Sherry

Combine apples and sherry in a container with a lid, and refrigerate for 5 days. Strain into a bottle with a cap and keep refrigerated.

GRAPPA & LEMON INFUSED DRY VERMOUTH

4 strips lemon peel
3 oz. (90 ml) grappa
2 cups dry vermouth

Place the lemon peel in a clean fancy bottle or clear wine bottle. Add the grappa and dry vermouth. Seal tightly. Let sit for a minimum of 24 hours before using so the lemon flavor develops. Store refrigerated for up to 1 month.

VERMOUTH DE PROVENCE

2 tbsp. Herbes de Provence
1 liter Noilly Prat extra-dry vermouth

Place the herbs in a small saucepan on medium heat for 2 minutes. Add 2 cups (480 ml) vermouth. Bring to a boil and immediately remove from the heat. Let stand until cool. Add the remaining vermouth and strain through a cheesecloth. Bottle and store at room temperature.

HOUSE ORANGE BITTERS

It's an old concept that's finding its way back into the bar: Making bitters that suit yours and customers' palates. For Audrey's Fitty-Fitty, her Pegu House Bitters blends Regan's Orange Bitters with Fee Brothers Orange Bitters to achieve the citrus level and complexity that she wanted

SYRUPS & WATERS

HONEY WATER

1.5 tbsp. honey (use a darker, better-grade honey if possible)
16 oz. (480 ml) water

Heat water in a saucepan to a low boil and stir in honey. Cool and store in a sealed glass container in the refrigerator until ready to use.

SPICED TEA SYRUP

1 cup (240 ml) water
18 whole cloves
1 Darjeeling tea bag
1 cup superfine sugar (200 gr)
½ tsp. ground cinnamon
½ tsp. pure vanilla extract

Bring water and cloves to a boil in a small pot and remove from heat. Add the tea bag and steep for about 5 minutes. Return to the heat and add sugar and cinnamon. Heat and stir until the sugar is dissolved. Remove from heat and add the vanilla extract. Strain through a coffee filter. Cool and store in the refrigerator in a tightly sealed glass jar until ready to use.

RASPBERRY SYRUP

400 gr fresh raspberries
2 cups (480 ml) water
250-400 gr superfine sugar, to taste

Place berries and water in a saucepan. Slowly bring to a boil on medium heat. When berries are extremely soft (about 2 to 3 minutes), strain through a coarse sieve and gently push through to release some of the pulp without getting loads of seeds. Add sugar to taste and return to the heat to dissolve. Strain into a mason jar or Kilner bottle while it's still hot and tightly seal it. Turn upside down in a bowl to let it cool. (This allows the heat to securely sterilize the top and seal it.)

At the height of the eighteenth-century gin craze, one out of every four habitable structures in the city of London housed a working gin still.

Zen Martini: A Martini with no vermouth at all. And no gin either.

—P. J. O'Rourke

The original food pairing for gin, starting shortly after the birth of English gin, was gingerbread.

The Martini naturally lends itself to the full spectrum of garnishes as it is neither sweet nor savory. Despite its complex taste, it has a neutral balance that can tip either way. An oversize peel from an especially sweet lemon or orange and it becomes a sweet drink. A bit of extra olive brine and it is deep and meaty. Just remember how much you paid for the good gin in that glass, and do it the honor of a high-quality garnish. A foie-gras-stuffed olive? A spoonful of caviar embedded in a vermouth jelly? Luxuries are ideal in small quantities. The garnish is a small quantity.

CLEMENTINE SYRUP

1 cup (240 ml) fresh clementine juice
1 oz. (30ml) fresh lemon juice
⅔ cup (135 gr) superfine sugar
1 clementine, sliced

Place all ingredients in a saucepan and slowly bring to a boil on medium heat. Turn the heat down to low and simmer for about 5 minutes. Strain into a mason jar or Kilner bottle while it's still hot and tightly seal it. Turn upside down in a bowl to let it cool. (This allows the heat to securely sterilize the top and seal it.)

GARNISHES

LEMON, ROSEMARY & GARLIC MARINATED OLIVES

5 large fresh rosemary sprigs
4 garlic cloves, thinly sliced
2 cups stuffed olives, drained
2 tbsp. olive oil
1 large lemon, cut into thin slices

Lay rosemary sprigs and garlic slices in an 8 x 8–inch glass dish. Then add the olives. Drizzle with the olive oil. Lay the lemon slices over the olives. Cover with plastic wrap and let marinate refrigerated for a minimum of 2 days before serving. Store refrigerated for up to 3 weeks.

PRESERVED PETALS

If you want to garnish your drink with flowers or petals, make sure they're pesticide-free. Some high-end grocery stores and farmers' markets sell edible flowers. Nasturtiums are pretty good; so are roses, violets, and daisies (avoid the bitter yellow centers). They can be used fresh or preserved.

To preserve petals for garnish, cover the bottom of a small bowl with sugar. Place the petals on the sugar so they're not touching each other. Cover them with more sugar and let them sit for a few days in a cool, dry place. To make sugar-encrusted "candied" petals, brush them with a little pasteurized egg white.

For a savory garnish, try the Japanese approach: Bury each flower in salt on a plate, and press them with another plate on top for a day. Rinse petals briefly under hot water before use.

Now get into the kitchen and let your imagination run rampant!

CHAPTER FOUR

R.S.V.P.

MARTINI PARTY PLANNING

Martinis have been the life of the party since the 1860s, when ostentatious banquets were held for just about every occasion. (Victorian etiquette dictated that our great-grandparents had to have a reason to throw a party.) Devil-may-care Jazz Babies and Bright Young Things during the Cocktail Age preferred death to missing a good cocktail party (or being seen at a boring one). The early 1960s were an era when posh little get-togethers were part of urban and suburban tribal tradition—a sign of good breeding.

Fortunately, you don't need an excuse—or peer pressure—to gather friends together at your home to tip a few glasses. Serving Martinis for more than four people is enough cause for a celebration. So how do you throw a hot party? A big budget's not required, but organization, inspiration, and perfect presentation are. So let's map out a few details.

The minister was booming away from the pulpit on the evils of alcohol. "Name one thing that's worse than drink!"

"Thirst," came a reply from the back row.

The first order of business is to pick a date. Experience has taught us not to schedule at-home fêtes during the work week unless you plan to hire a caterer to set up, serve, and clean up the remnants of your soirée. Fridays and Saturdays are the best days. They give you and your guests a chance to recuperate from the festivities. (You could add a bunch of cheap sunglasses to your party favors list so people can leave your abode at dawn in style. Plus, putting the whole party in shades adds a really amusing air of instant cool.)

PARTY TYPES

Once you've pinpointed the party date, it's time to make your biggest decision: What type of Martini party should you throw? Here are a few thoughts to get you started:

A sophisticated cocktail party—like something out of a feature film like *All About Eve* or *La Dolce Vita*—is ideal if you and your friends love dressing up in formal wear, tipping toasts with your best stemware, and—optionally—puffing the finest cigars and cigarettes.

A classy little come-as-you-are cocktail affair straight out of the pages of a Cocktail Age Dashiell Hammett mystery or P. G. Wodehouse comedy is just the thing if your guests are coming over straight from work, going to a gala, cocktail hopping, or tearing themselves away from the television. For a few hours, the gang can kick up their heels to some Cotton Club jazz or wax philosophic about Hemingway adventures and basketball over a few masterfully mixed shakerfuls in your (living room) salon.

If the forecast calls for warm and sunny, you might want to throw a pool or even a rooftop party. Take a look at back *Playboy* issues from the 1960s for inspiration. The lineup of sports cars parked in front of your house and the bevy of babes in bikinis and cocktail dresses sauntering around the backyard will keep your neighbors talking till winter, especially if one of your guests performs some of the poolside antics from that film tribute to Swinging London style, *Scandal,* or every James Bond film Sean Connery made.

One of our favorite party accessories is a Twister board. For larger parties, put two of them side by side. If you're hosting a pool party, it's the ultimate way to make sure everyone's wearing sunblock. Just spill a whole bottle out onto the Twister board and watch how quickly everyone gets covered. Now send out those invitations!

PARTY SUPPLIES

Before you stock up on your Martini party supplies, write your drink menu. Once you know how many guests are coming, start nailing down your recipes and then your shopping list.

The math is simple: you get fourteen 2 oz. pours of gin or vodka per 750 ml bottle. Let's say twelve guests are coming who seem to have a three-Martini limit. Subtracting a couple of designated drivers, you need to buy three bottles of gin or vodka or two bottles of each. (You'll either be rewarded with a leftover portion or the knowledge no one's calling you a dry well behind your back.)

Tag on one bottle of dry vermouth (that's fifty 0.5 oz. servings or just under 7,000 drops per 750 ml bottle) and a bottle of each item (orange juice, Cointreau, champagne, liqueur, scotch, etc.) needed to mix your menu. Remember, you can get away with small bottles of many of these.

There're two jokers in every deck and at least one in every crowd, so here's a harmless practical joke for cocktail parties:

Buy a small package of Knox (clear) gelatin. Mix according to the instructions, substituting your regular proportions of gin and vermouth for half the water called for. As soon as it's ready, pour it over an olive or twist in a Martini glass, and put it in the fridge to chill.

When you're mixing drinks for your guests wait until the second or third round, then pour a tiny bit of fresh Martini on top of it and hand that one to someone as if it's a regular drink. If you're not serving at home, chances are you can get your favorite bartender to conspire with you if you set it up a day or two in advance.

BASIC CRUDITÉ DIP

Makes 4 to 6 appetizer servings

1 cup sour cream

2 tbsp. horseradish

1 tbsp. finely chopped chives or scallions

Combine all ingredients in a bowl and mix thoroughly. Serve with bite-size pieces of carrot, blanched broccoli or asparagus, celery, green beans, individual endive leaves, or any other vegetable you prefer.

ROASTED GARLIC

Makes 2 to 4 appetizer servings

1 head garlic

3 tablespoons extra-virgin olive oil

Do not peel the garlic. Simply cut the top off to expose the tops of the individual cloves. Place on a foil-covered baking sheet, drizzle oil on top, and bake in a preheated 350°F oven for 45 minutes to an hour. Serve hot or cold.

Top your list with necessary garnishes—olives, pickled onions, lemons, oranges, etc.—and any requisite bar tools you might be missing, like an extra cocktail shaker or mixing glass and cup with strainer, jiggers or shot glasses (one to accompany each shaker), Martini glasses (at least two per guest, though we prefer to have a few extras), and a couple of ice buckets filled with ice.

PARTY FOOD

Even we have to admit that men and women can't live by Martinis alone; they must have munchies. But we would never masticate conventional potato chips and pretzels while sipping our favorite elixirs. And we would never serve such mundane morsels to our Martini-savvy guests. The idea is to serve foods that'll reach an anesthetized palate without overwhelming it. With that in mind, we've developed a master list of single-handed finger food that we find ourselves reaching for before the throngs arrive:

- A selection of olives in a variety of sizes, stuffings, and marinades as well as some cocktail onions
- Mixed nuts, Terra Chips, Kettle Chips (not your ordinary chips, please)
- A platter of cheeses like Roquefort, Stilton, sharp cheddar, and port wine cheddar (skip the Brie and Gouda, they don't do so well with Martinis)
- Peppery cheese sticks
- Roasted garlic (see recipe on this page)
- Crudité (raw veggies cut into bite-size pieces) served with a horseradish cream sauce (see recipe on this page)

- Pâté maison, chopped chicken liver, or duck terrine served with baguette slices and cornichons

- Skewers of shrimp or prawns dusted with a simple combo of spices (see recipe on this page) (Impress the socks off your friends by putting one shrimp on each skewer, then stab the back ends into a pineapple sliced diagonally to make a simple bouquet.)

- Platter of steamed or fried dumplings delivered from the nearest Chinese restaurant

- Medallions of rare roast beef served on toast rounds and topped with Béarnaise sauce

- Miniature potato and scallion pancakes topped with sour cream

- Smoked salmon platter served with capers, minced red onion, and bread rounds

- Raw oysters served on the half shell with fresh lemon wedges

- Caviar served with chopped egg, minced white onion, lemon wedges, and toast points

- Scallops or water chestnuts wrapped in pancetta (or regular bacon) that are skewered and grilled

- Miniature tart shells filled with curried chicken and topped with toasted walnuts and champagne grapes

- Toasted Italian bread slices topped with chopped fresh plum tomatoes, chopped garlic, extra-virgin olive oil, wilted spinach, salt and pepper (aka: Bruschetta Florentina)

- Miniature tart shells filled with whole pecans and a pecan-pie glaze flavored with chocolate liqueur

EASY CAJUN SHRIMP BOUQUET

Makes 5 appetizer servings

½ tbsp. salt

1 tsp. ground black pepper

½ tsp. ground cayenne pepper

½ tsp. garlic powder

1 lb. fresh medium-size shrimp (about 30)

1 whole, fresh pineapple

Combine all dry ingredients in a salt shaker and set aside. Peel and devein shrimp. Place the shrimp on the tips of individual 8-10" bamboo skewers. Bring 3 cups of water to a boil. Place skewers into the water, shrimp end down. Reduce heat to medium and boil for 3 minutes. Slice the pineapple diagonally from the bottom to midway up the opposite side so that it will sit at an angle on a plate (leave the top on).

Remove the shrimp from the water, dust with the seasoning mix, and then stick the other ends of the skewers into the pineapple.

FOOD COCKTAILS

While you're playing in the kitchen, you might as well experiment with a few foods that can be served in Martini glasses: an equally elegant accompaniment for sit-down soirées. The simplest snack to serve "up" is olives. Shake up an extra Martini and then pour a quarter of it over a glass filled with olives. This ensures that the drink and snack flavors match. (The best Martinis for this are the ones made with gin or vodka and vermouth. Otherwise, you may find yourself tossing out olives.)

A more elegant dish is Drunken Prawns: prawns steamed in a mixture of vodka, gin, pickled ginger, salt, and pepper. The nice thing about prawns (or shrimp with cocktail sauce, which is just a mixture of ketchup and horseradish) is that you can hook them around the rim of the glass, and for the few minutes it might take, you can look like you studied cooking at Le Cordon Bleu. Even salsa looks better in a Martini glass (and tortilla chips are surprisingly well designed to reach the bottom). It can be garnished with a wedge of lime on the rim, or a few chips stuck around the edge.

- Fresh whole strawberries served with a small bowl of sour cream flavored with a pinch of ground cinnamon and dark brown sugar for dipping

Obviously you're not expected to serve everything on this list. We don't. The idea is to pick a couple of the basics and a couple of fancier dishes. Or, if you're not into cooking but someone who's coming is, you can always see if you can talk them into making one of these for you.

So where do you find the best moments that the cocktail culture has to offer? As one New Yorker who had a habit of crashing every party she passed on the street (and often got invited back for the next one) said, "Great moments aren't found. They're made."

SHAKEN NOT STIRRED

So Strut Your Stuff

ONLY 4,278 MILES TO
WALL DRUG
of South Dakota, U.S.A.
from HARRY'S

CHAPTER FIVE

HAPPY HOUR

SOME OF THE WORLD'S BEST MARTINI BARS

No matter where you go, chances are you can find a good Martini or two these days if you know where to look. Thanks to the revival of lounge culture (and innumerable subcultures), new watering holes are cropping up every month. We suggest that you visit the Web site World's Best Bars (www.worldsbestbars.com) to locate a pit stop that suits your mood and locale. The establishments we've listed here are ones that we've personally spent many happy hours in, and others that were highly recommended by our esteemed mixological colleagues.

What is it that makes a bar, restaurant, or hotel bar ideal for Martini drinking? A talented mixologist and a bar team that believes the customer comes first, obvious care in stocking both premium spirits and fresh ingredients, and comfortable surroundings are high on our checklist. We also tend to walk into a place we've never been before and ask for a Martini—the ultimate test of a bartender's skill and attention to service all rolled into one.

ICON KEY

A recipe from this establishment is featured in the text.

Cocktail lounge: A half-lit room full of half-lit people.

—Robert Meyers

CANADA

🍸 **900 West,** Fairmont Hotel, 900 W. Georgia, Vancouver, BC V6C 2W6

Bar None, 1222 Hamilton Street, Vancouver, BC V6B 2S8

George Lounge, 1137 Hamilton Street, Vancouver, BC V6B 5P6

Le LAB, 1351 rue Rachel Est., Montreal, QUE H2J 2K2

Martini Club, 103–55 Mill Street, Toronto, ONT M5A 3C4

The Keno Lounge, The Westmark Hotel, Fifth & Harper Streets, Dawson City, Yukon Y0B 1G0

FRANCE

Bar Le Forum, 4 Boulevard Malesherbes, Paris 75008

Curio Parlor, 16, rue des Bernardins, Paris 75005

Experimental Cocktail Club, 37 rue Saint-Sauveur, Paris, 75002

🍸 Harry's New York Bar, 5 rue Danau, Paris 75002

Hemingway Bar, Ritz Hotel, 15 Place Vendôme, Paris 75001

Bar 228, Hotel Le Meurice, 228 rue de Rivoli, Paris 75001

GERMANY

Le Lion—Bar de Paris, Rathausstraße 3 20095 Hamburg

Leibenstern—Bar im Einstein, Café Einstein Stammhaus, Kurfürstenstraße 58, 10785 Berlin

🍸 Mauro's Negroni Club, Kellerstraße 32, 81667 Munich

Schumann's Bar, Odeonplatz 6+7, 80539 Munich

The Martini Club, Theresienstrasse 93, D-80333 Munich

Victoria Bar, Potsdamerstraße 102, 10785 Berlin

GREAT BRITAIN

🍸 American Bar at the Savoy Hotel, Strand, London WC2R 0EU

Artesian Bar, The Langham Hotel, 1 Portland Place, London, W1B 1JA

Connaught Bar, The Connaught, Carlos Place, London W1K 2AL

🍸 Dukes Bar, Dukes Hotel, St. James's Place, London SW1A 1NY

🍸 Hawksmoor at Seven Dials, 11 Langley Street, London WC2H 9JG

Mark's Bar, HIX Soho, 70 Brewer Street, London W1F 9

Portobello Star, 171 Portobello Road, Notting Hill, London W11 2DY

Raoul's Cocktail Bar, 32 Walton Street, Oxford OX2 6AA

GREECE

42 Bar, Kolokotroni 3, 10562 Athens

A for Athens Hotel, Top Floor, 2–4, Miaouli, Monastiraki, 10554 Athens

Baba au Rhum, 6 Kleitiou, 10560 Athens

The Gin Joint, Lada Christou 1, 10561 Athens

ITALY

Stravinskj Bar, Hotel de Russie, Via del Babuino 9, Rome 00187

Victoria Cafe, 1 Via Clerici, Milan 20121 .

Yar, Via Mercalli 22, Milan 20122.

JAPAN

🍸 **Bar High Five,** 4th Floor, No. 26 Polestar Building, 7–2–14 Ginza, Tokyo

Old Imperial Bar, Imperial Hotel, 1–1–1 Uchisaiwaicho, Tokyo

Star Bar Ginza, Sankosha Building B1F, 1–5–13 Ginza, Tokyo

NETHERLANDS

Door 74, 74 Reguliersdwarsstraat, Amsterdam 1017 BN

Vesper Bar, 57 Vinkenstraat, Amsterdam 1013 JM

RUSSIAN FEDERATION

Chaika, 7 Marksistskaya Ulitsa, Moscow

Dream Bar, 17/1 Myasnit-skaya Ulitsa, Moscow

Noor Bar, 23 Tverskaya Ulitsa, Moscow

SCOTLAND

Bramble Bar & Lounge, 16a Queen Street, Edinburgh EH2 1JE

Tonic, 34a North Castle Street, New Town, Edinburgh EH2 3BN

SLOVAKIA

Lemontree & Sky Bar, viezdoslavovo nám 189/7 81102 Bratislava

🍸 **Paparazzi,** Laurinská 133/1 811 01 Bratislava

SPAIN

Dry Martini Bar, Carrer Aribau 162–166, Eixample, Barcelona 08036

🍸 **Bar Boadas,** Tallers 1, Barcelona 08001

Ideal Bar, 89 Carrer Aribau (at Carrer de Mallorca), Barcelona 08036

Milano Cocktail Bar, 35 Ronda Universidad, Barcelona 08007

Tirsa Bar, 174 Carrer Rafael de Campalans, L'Hospitalet, Barcelona 08903

THE UNITED STATES

🍸 **'21' Club,** 21 West Fifty-second Street, New York, NY 11019

Balcony Club, 1825 Abrams Road, Dallas, TX 75214

🍸 **Bar Marmont,** The Chateau Marmont, 8221 Sunset Boulevard, Hollywood, CA 90046

Bardot Speakeasy, 3456 N. Miami Ave, Miami, FL 33127

🍸 **Bemelman's Bar,** 35 East Seventy-sixth Street New York, NY 10021

Bix Restaurant and Supper Club, 56 Gold Street, San Francisco, CA 94133

Blue Wasabi Sushi & Martini Bar, 6137 North Scottsdale Road, Scottsdale, AZ 85250

Bourbon & Branch, 501 Jones Street, San Francisco, CA 94102

Carousel Bar, Hotel Monteleone, 214 Rue Royale, New Orleans, LA 70130

Clover Club, 210 Smith Street, Brooklyn NY 11201

Death + Company, 433 East Sixth Street, New York, NY 10009

Delano Hotel, 1685 Collins Avenue, Miami, FL 33139

Employees Only, 510 Hudson Street, New York, NY 10014

Fez, 3815 N. Central Avenue, Phoenix, AZ 85012

French 75 Bar, 813 Bienville Street New Orleans, LA 70112

Harry Denton's Starlight Room, 450 Powell Street, San Francisco, CA 94108

Little Branch, 22 Seventh Avenue South, New York, NY 10014

Lola's Restaurant, 945 North Fairfax Avenue, West Hollywood, CA 90046

Martini Bar, Millennium Knickerbocker Hotel Chicago, 163 East Walton Place, Chicago, IL 60611

Martini Bar, The Raleigh Hotel, 1775 Collins Avenue, Miami Beach, FL 33139

Metropolitan Grill, 820 Second Avenue, Seattle, WA 98104

Mint/820, 816 North Russell Street, Portland, OR 97227

Musso & Frank Grill, 6667 Hollywood Boulevard, Los Angeles, CA 90028

Oliver's, Mayflower Park Hotel, 405 Olive Way, Seattle, WA 98101

Pegu Club, 77 West Houston Street, New York, NY 10012

Pravda, 281 Lafayette Street, New York, NY 10003

The Dresden Room, 1760 North Vermont Avenue, Los Angeles, CA 90027

The Edison, 108 West Second Street, Los Angeles, CA 90012

The Four Seasons Restaurant, 99 E. Fifty-second Street, New York, NY 10022

The Gibson, 2009 Fourteenth Street, Washington, D.C. 20009

The Ivy, 113 N Roberston Boulevard, Los Angeles, CA 90048

The Redwood Room, The Clift Hotel, 495 Geary Street, San Francisco, CA 94102

The Round Robin, The Willard Intercontinental Hotel, 1401 Pennsylvania Avenue, Washington D.C., 20004

The Varnish, behind Cole's Bar, 118 East Sixth Street, Los Angeles, CA 90014

The Violet Hour, 1520 North Damen Avenue, Chicago, IL 60622

Zig Zag Café, 1501 Western Avenue, Seattle, WA 98101

SELECTED BIBLIOGRAPHY

Amis, Kingsley. *On Drink.* (New York: Harcourt Brace Jovanovich, Inc., 1970 and 1972).

Asbury, Herbert (ed.), and Jerry Thomas. *The Bon Vivant's Companion.* (New York: Alfred A. Knopf, 1928).

Blom, Eric (ed.). *Grove's Dictionary of Music and Musicians,* vol. V. (London: Macmillan & Co. Ltd., 1954).

Bredenbek, Magnus. *What Shall We Drink?* (New York: Carlyle House, 1934).

Browne, Charles. *The Gun Club Drink Book.* (New York: Charles Scribner's Sons, 1939).

Coward, Noël. *Autobiography.* (London: Methuen Ltd., 1986).

Doxat, John. *Stirred Not Shaken: The Dry Martini.* (London: Hutchinson Benham Ltd., 1976).

———. *The Book of Drinking.* (London: Tribune Books, 1973).

Edwards, Bill. *How to Mix Drinks.* (Philadelphia: David McKay Company, 1936).

Feery, William C. *Wet Drinks for Dry People.* (New York: William C. Ferry, 1932).

Fleming, Ian. *Casino Royale.* (London: Glidrose Productions Ltd., 1952).

———. *Thrilling Cities.* (London: Glidrose Productions Ltd., 1964).

———. *You Only Live Twice.* (London: Glidrose Productions Ltd., 1964).

Flexner, Stuart Berg. *Listening to America: An Illustrated History of Words and Phrases from Our Lively and Splendid Past.* (New York: Simon & Schuster, 1982).

Gaige, Crosby. *The Standard Cocktail Guide: A Manual of Mixed Drinks Written for the American Host.* (New York: M. Barrows & Co., 1944).

Hemingway, Ernest. *A Farewell to Arms.* (New York: Charles Scribner's Sons, 1929).

———. *Islands in the Stream.* (London: William Collins Sons & Co., Ltd., 1970).

Herter, George Leonard, and Berthe Herter. *Bull Cook and Authentic Historical Recipes and Practices.* (Waseca, MN: Herter's, 1963).

Johnson, Harry. *New and Improved Illustrated Bartender's Manual or How to Mix Drinks of the Present Style.* (New York: Harry Johnson, 1882).

Lycett, Andrew. *Ian Fleming.* (London: Weidenfeld & Nicholson, 1995).

Mailer, Norman. *Harlot's Ghost.* (New York: Harcourt Brace Jovanovich, 1991).

Mariani, John. *America Eats Out: An Illustrated History of Restaurants, Taverns, Coffee Shops, Speakeasies, and Other Establishments That Have Fed Us for 350 Years.* (New York: William Morrow & Co., Inc., 1991).

Mario, Thomas. *Playboy's Host & Bar Book.* (Chicago: Playboy Press, 1971).

Marx, Harpo, and Rowland Barber. *Harpo Speaks!* (New York: Limelight Editions, 1985).

Mason, Dexter. *The Art of Drinking or What to Make with What You Have.* (New York: Farrar & Rinehart, 1930).

Mencken, H. L. *The American Language: An Inquiry into the Development of English in the United States,* 4th ed. (New York: Alfred A. Knopf, 1963).

Oscar of the Waldorf, *101 Famous Cocktails.* (New York: Kenilworth Press, 1934).

Smith, Martin Cruz. *Polar Star.* (New York: Ballantine Books, 1989).

Thomas, Jerry. *The Bar-Tender's Guide and the Bon Vivant's Companion.* (New York: Dick & Fitzgerald Publishers, 1862).

Watney, John. *Mother's Ruin: A History of Gin.* (London: Peter Owen, Ltd., 1976).

White, Francesca. *Cheers! A Spirited Guide to Liquors and Liqueurs.* (London: Paddington Press, 1977).

Wiley, James E. *The Art of Mixing.* (Philadelphia: Macrae Smith Co., 1932).

Wodehouse, P. G. *Mulliner Nights.* (London: H. Jenkins, 1966).

INDEX

PERMISSIONS

LAST CALL

When Bill passed away, he was surprised to find himself facing the Pearly Gates. "I always thought Martini drinkers went the other direction," he remarked to St. Peter.

"Who'd you think invented the Martini? Professor Jerry Thomas? It is truly a Divine Inspiration," St. Peter chuckled, leading the newcomer off on a heavenly cook's tour.

Soon they entered the biggest room Bill had ever seen: The walls were covered from floor to ceiling with clocks. "These are the Life Clocks," the saint pointed out. "They measure every aspect of life performed by every living thing. For instance, every time you ate breakfast, the second hand on your Life Clock ticked.

"And these," St. Peter remarked when they passed the Cocktail Clocks, "mark every time you've had a cocktail, or even thought about it."

"Where's mine?" Bill asked. They looked all around, but couldn't find it. So St. Peter wandered off to ask one of the attending angels.

"It seems yours is upstairs," St. Peter said when he returned. "Somebody was using it as a fan."

ABOUT THE AUTHORS

Drink historians and recipients of the 2011 International Wine & Spirits Competition Communicator of the Year Award, Jared Brown and Anistatia Miller have written more than thirty books during their twenty-year collaboration, including *Shaken Not Stirred®: A Celebration of the Martini, The Mixellany Guide to Vermouth & Other Apéritifs,* and *Cuban Cocktails.* Their two-volume *Spirituous Journey: A History of Drink* charts the history of spirits and mixed drinks from 7000 B.C. to the mid-twentieth century. (The first volume won a coveted Gourmand World Cookbook Award for Best Drink History in the UK in 2009 and the second received the same honor in 2010.) And in October 2010, the couple also received the Best Drinks Writing Award at the 2010 CLASS Magazine Awards.

Miller and Brown are contributing editors for World's Best Bars and are "cocktail gurus" on *Drinkology.* They are also regular contributors to *Imbibe* and *CLASS* magazines in the UK and *Mixology* magazine in Germany. They have written extensively for other publications, including *Wine Spectator, Cigar Aficionado, Gotham* and *Hamptons* magazines, *Los Angeles Confidential, Boston Common, Capitol File,* and *Food Arts* in the United States as well as *THEME* and *Imbibe* in the UK.

These two former bartenders also practice what they preach. Brown is master distiller for the multi-award-winning Sipsmith Gin, the first newly licensed London distillery to open in nearly two hundred years. They have amassed a collection of international awards for their work as distillery consultants creating new spirits, including a coveted 2002 international "Best Spirit" in the white spirits category from the Beverage Testing Institute for Heavy Water Vodka. They have worked as tasters for a number of products, including the Beefeater 24 and No. 3 Gin. They recently completed a three-year project in the South of France, restoring Exposition Universelle des Vins et Spiritueux, a museum of wines and spirits founded in 1958, and cataloging the 8,000+ bottles, 1,200 menus, and other antiquities in the collection.

They live in the Cotswolds with their cat, Kitten.